The Accidental Trainer

The Accidental Trainer

You Know Computers, So They Want You To Teach Everyone Else

Elaine Weiss

Jossey-Bass Publishers • San Francisco

Jossey-Bass books and products are available through most bookstores. To contact Jossey-Bass directly, call (888) 378-2537, fax to (800) 605-2665, or visit our website at www.josseybass.com.

Substantial discounts on bulk quantities of Jossey-Bass books are available to corporations, professional associations, and other organizations. For details and discount information, contact the special sales department at Jossey-Bass.

Library of Congress Cataloging-in-Publication Data

Weiss, Elaine, date.
  The accidental trainer : you know computers, so they want you to teach everyone else / Elaine Weiss.
      p. cm. — (Jossey-Bass business & management series)
  Includes bibliographical references and index.
  ISBN 0-7879-0293-4
  1. Electronic data processing—Study and teaching. I. Title. II. Series
QA76.27.W434 1997
004'.071'5—dc20   96-16106

FIRST EDITION
PB Printing   10 9 8 7 6 5 4 3 2

**The Jossey-Bass
Business & Management Series**

Contents

Section Four: How Can I Tell If It Worked?

Preface

Chances are you never planned to become a trainer. Most people don't. Trainers, especially computer trainers, tend to fall into the role accidentally. First they are simply resident experts: having mastered a few software programs, they enjoy sharing their knowledge with anyone who shows even a speck of interest. Since technology is fun for them, they take pride in conquering a program's quirks and complexities. Then word gets out, and before long they are the ones whose phones ring when the system crashes. And one morning they wake up to discover that they are doing more than giving advice; they are teaching. They have become computer trainers.

In the book *How to Be a Jewish Mother*,[1] Dan Greenberg explains that you don't have to be Jewish (or a mother, for that matter) to be a Jewish Mother. Intent, not heritage, confers the title: if you behave like a Jewish Mother, you are a Jewish Mother. The same logic applies to computer trainers. Though your official job description may be quite different, if you teach people to use computers, you are a computer trainer. The data entry clerk at a Wall Street brokerage firm, who shows all her co-workers how to generate weekly usage reports, is a computer trainer. So is the managing editor of a monthly magazine, whom everyone calls when they stumble over the company's E-mail system.

If you have made the leap from resident expert to computer trainer, this book is for you. It will show you how to create effective training for computer users—training that is clear, concise, on target, and memorable. It will show you how to get your students up to speed in a minimum of time, with a minimum of pain. Sometimes this training will happen in a classroom. Much of the time it will happen at an individual learner's desk. Wherever it is located, the goal is the same: to get people and technology to work together.

As a computer trainer, you are in the business of building bridges—in this case, educational structures that span the gap between people and technology. Imagine a wide, fast-flowing river. Piled in a heap on one side of the river is all the technology in which your organization has invested. This pile grows larger every year (for example, the percentage of U.S. workers using computers on the job increased from 25 percent in 1984 to 47 percent in 1993).[2] On the other side of the river, bunched together on the muddy bank, are all the people who need to use that technology. A few brave souls plunge into the river and swim across on their own, to emerge dripping but safe on the other side. These folks can obviously fend for themselves. But that still leaves a hefty crowd to move across the river—and they can't swim. Your job is to build the bridge that gets the people across the river to the technology. If there are a lot of people, you may have to build several bridges. If the river is infested with alligators, such as resistance to change, your bridge must be particularly robust. If money and time are tight, you may have to make do with a tightrope, but a few people (especially those who are afraid of heights) will probably fall into the river and get swept downstream.

One thing is certain: building a bridge is a tricky task. It takes planning, as well as a good understanding of engineering principles. Building an educational bridge between people and technology is equally tricky. Whether you are responsible for training one person or several hundred, the questions are the same. How much information can be presented without overwhelming the learners? What is the best way to challenge learners without intimidating them? How can users be encouraged to read the user manual? When is it appropriate to evaluate training, and what should be measured? If you are like most accidental trainers, you never formally learned how to teach; everything you know about the teaching-learning process you picked up along the way. This book will help you approach the task in a more orderly manner.

Section One contains two chapters that present the challenges faced by computer trainers. Chapter One describes what happens when unconsciously competent teachers meet consciously incompetent students—what can go wrong, and how you can make it right. Chapter Two takes you on a quick tour of the blueprint for computer training that is explored in detail in the remainder of the book.

Sections Two, Three, and Four help you answer three key questions about how to create effective computer training:

- What do I teach?
- How do I teach it?
- How can I tell if it worked?

Section Two addresses the first of these questions: "What do I teach?" Its focus is on content. The three chapters in this section describe how you can assess the learner, the system, and the job to ensure that your training is on target. Chapter Three describes different types of learners, and explains how to target your training to meet the diverse needs of each type. Chapter Four shows you how to evaluate the strengths and weaknesses of a computer system so that you can target your training to the parts of the system that may create learning and usage problems. Chapter Five explores how computer training fits into the larger context of the organization, and explains how to target your training to the skills that learners are most likely to use on the job.

Section Three considers the second question: "How do I teach it?" The two chapters in this section address process—specifically, the teaching-learning process. Chapter Six examines how people learn and how effective teachers teach. It summarizes the current thinking on the mental processes people use when they acquire new information, and describes the conditions that must be in place for learners to remember what they are taught. The chapter then presents instructional techniques that you can use to make your training sessions productive and enjoyable for your learners. Chapter Seven discusses the importance of using instructional materials to support and supplement the learning process. Because you can never teach it all, and because your students can never learn it all, this chapter shows you when and how to develop support materials that learners can use both during and after training.

Section Four tackles the third, and trickiest, question: "How can I tell if it worked?" This section examines issues of outcome. In a speech to Williams College alumni in 1871, President James Garfield described education as a student at one end of a bench and a teacher at the other end. If you want to discover whether your training has been effective, you need to examine what is going on at each end of the bench. Chapter Eight describes how to evaluate teaching. It explains how to use student attitude surveys, peer review, and self-assessment to determine the quality of the instruction. Chapter Nine describes how to evaluate learning. It discusses ways to assess how learners feel, what they know, and what they can do as a result of your teaching.

Teaching is a complex activity. As a student, you were probably disappointed by well-meaning but ineffective teachers. Now that the shoe is on the other foot, you want (but don't quite know how) to do better. How do you transfer all that good knowledge from your head into the heads of your learners? Hundreds of people have written thousands of useful pages on this subject. While these writings are valuable resources, chances are that you have neither the time, energy, nor inclination to study them. The sculptor Brancusi wrote: "Simplicity is complexity resolved."[3] This book aims to simplify: to synthesize the complex process of teaching, making it accessible to accidental trainers. I hope you find it helpful.

Speaking of helpfulness, several people have been especially helpful as this book has evolved. At Jossey-Bass, Sarah Polster's initial encouragement gave me the courage to tackle a second book. Editors Bill Hicks and Larry Alexander provided excellent guidance and direction. I also want to thank Celia Weiss, my mother and copyeditor par excellence, who, from the time I was old enough to pick up a pencil, taught me to pay attention to the details. Finally, again and always, I am grateful to my husband, Neal Whitman, for doing what he does best: the perfect balance of critical reading, insightful thinking, and steadfast moral support.

Salt Lake City, Utah   Elaine Weiss
August 1996

This book is dedicated
to the ones I love best

my mother, *Celia Weiss*
and
my husband, *Neal Whitman*

The Author

Elaine Weiss has been an instructional design consultant since 1975. After seven years designing and delivering a wide variety of corporate training programs, she developed her first computer-use course in 1981. Since that time, her mission in life has been to make good things happen between people and computers.

To support the "human" side of human-computer interactions, Weiss makes people computer-literate (by developing courses, tutorials, job aids, and user guides) and makes computers people-literate (by defining user requirements and designing user interfaces).

Her consulting practice has spanned such industries as banking, brokerage services, communications, health care, insurance, and manufacturing. Clients have included AT&T, The American Heart Association, Corning Glass, General Electric, Lincoln National Corporation, Market Data Corporation, Pacific First Bank, and Security-Connecticut Life, among others.

The author is a member of the American Society for Training and Development (ASTD), the Society for Technical Communication (STC), and the Association for Computing Machinery (ACM). From 1992 to 1994 she was the topic editor for the NSPI book series *From Training to Performance in the Twenty-First Century*.

Weiss received her Ed.D. degree in instructional design from Columbia University. She is the author of *Making Computers*

People-Literate (Jossey-Bass, 1994) and has contributed articles to professional publications. She also writes the popular "Computing For Poets" column in *Catalyst* magazine. Weiss is known for her ability to make complex concepts accessible and engaging for her readers.

The Accidental Trainer

SECTION ONE

Building Bridges Between
People and Computers

1

If You Teach People to Use Computers, Then This Book Is for You

If you teach people to use computers, you are in good company. The proliferation of technology in the workplace has made it mandatory for businesses to train their workers to make the most effective use of that technology. Nearly 90 percent of U.S. businesses provide formal training in the use of computers.[1] Of the more than $50 billion that U.S. companies spend annually on training, well over $5 billion are directed toward the users of information technology.[2]

If you teach people to use computers, you have your hands full. Technology is not only proliferating; it is also constantly changing. Computer hardware and software seem to become obsolete in a matter of months. Consequently, trained users don't stay trained. They need retraining every time the equipment gets fancier or the software gets upgraded. Simply keeping abreast of these changes can be a full-time job; carrying the word to end-users may feel overwhelming. It was simpler in the days when computers were gargantuan beasts tended by the elect few; while these workers certainly needed training (and retraining), there just weren't that many of them. These days, computers are everywhere. There were ten office workers to every display terminal in the early 1980s; by 1993 that ratio had dropped dramatically to two workers per terminal.[3] In 1995, nearly two-thirds of U.S. executives reported using computers in their jobs.[4]

If you teach people to use computers, you are doing critical work. Computer use has moved well beyond routine data entry. Hardware, software, and the people who use them have become incredibly sophisticated. Management guru Peter Drucker has predicted that by the year 2000, fully one-third of the U.S. workforce will be doing some form of "knowledge work." He believes that a significant element of the knowledge worker's expertise will be his or her ability to create, capture, manipulate, manage, and apply information.[5]

Finally, if you teach people to use computers, you may be wondering if you are up to the challenge. You may also be trying to remember how you got into this pickle in the first place. Chances are you did not wake up one morning when you were eight years old and say to yourself, "I don't think I'll be a firefighter after all. I think when I grow up I'll earn my living by teaching people to use computers." If you are like many computer trainers, you fell into the role accidentally. Perhaps you started out as the company's resident expert on the quirks of the E-mail system. Maybe you are the programmer who designed the system in the first place. You may not think of yourself as a techno-dweeb, but everyone views you that way because you know more than they do. And now, because you know computers, they want you to teach everyone else.

Overcoming the Competence Paradox

Don't panic! On the one hand, you are the best person for the job. After all, you have been asked to teach others precisely because you have a better grasp of computers than the people you will be teaching. This gives you enormous credibility with your students. On the other hand, the very knowledge that is your strength can also be your greatest handicap. To be an effective computer trainer, you need to be more than a power-user-in-front-of-a-group. The trouble with power users is that they have forgotten what it was like to be novices. Also, they are so excited about the system that they find it hard to relinquish control of the keyboard. So they sit down at the computer, saying, "Let me show you a few neat things," and learners' eyes glaze over as menus appear, screens disappear, windows move, and colors flash.

This behavior is due to the well-known "competence paradox": the people with the greatest skill are often the poorest teachers. Think of a championship tennis player. Her legs know precisely where to run to catch the ball at the last second, and her wrist knows exactly how to flick the ball back to an unretrievable corner of her opponent's court—but she has no idea how she does it. In other words, she is unconsciously competent.

Let's examine this issue of competence. Whenever people master a new skill, they go through four stages (see Figure 1.1). At the lowest level, unconscious incompetence, not only are you unable to perform a skill, you don't even know there is a skill to perform! At the next level, conscious incompetence, you still can't perform the skill, but you are aware of your inability. In other words, you know what you don't know. Unconsciously incompetent learners must reach conscious incompetence before they are ready to pay attention to a teacher.

FIGURE 1.1. Levels of Competence.

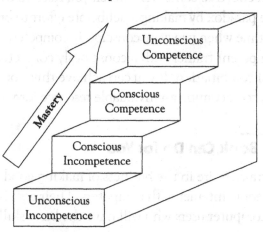

Immediately after you learn a skill, you are consciously competent. Although you can perform all the steps required to complete a task, you are aware of each step as you take it. For example, after moving to a new city, you learn how to get from your house to your office, but you pay careful attention to each street sign along your route. You may even mumble little cues to yourself as you drive: "There's the gas station: I have to turn right. Now I need to keep my eyes open for the big oak tree."

Finally, after you have fully mastered a skill, you are unconsciously competent. You get into your car, turn the key, and thirty minutes later you pull into your office parking lot with no conscious memory of having driven there. Not only can you perform the skill, but you can perform it on autopilot! And if someone from your office asks for directions to your house, you have a hard time coming up with a clear set of steps.

Now, in most companies, the people who are selected to be computer trainers are so familiar with the hardware and software that they have become unconsciously competent. The competence paradox, however, is that learners learn best from a consciously competent teacher. Someone who is consciously competent still remembers what it was like to struggle with a counterintuitive software program. He or she is aware of each substep required to turn on the computer, print a document, or fix a mistake.

To be an effective computer trainer, you need to overcome the competence paradox by making a deliberate effort to bring yourself back to the time when you were consciously competent. An unconsciously competent trainer with a consciously competent mind-set is a powerful combination. If you can achieve this, you will be well on your way to becoming an invaluable resource for your students.

What This Book Can Do for You

Computer trainers are in the business of making good things happen when people interact with computers. Their goal is to produce motivated computer users who will have the basic skills needed to apply what they learned, and who will continue learning back on the job.[6] This book will help you achieve this goal by showing you how to design and deliver training that is on target, understandable, and memorable. If people are more efficient, effective, and satisfied computer users as a result of your training, then you have been successful.

All the principles, guidelines, and suggestions in this book are designed to increase your success by improving your competence as a teacher. You may be consciously incompetent: you may know enough to know that you don't know how to teach, and your major concern may be what to do on Monday morning. Or you may be consciously competent: you may have done some teaching, and are looking for ways to be more effective. As you read this book, keep in mind that whether or not you have taught before, you already are experienced in one aspect of the teaching-learning process. You have spent years as a learner! As noted in the Preface, President James Garfield described education as a student at one end of a bench and a teacher at the other end. You already know what you like (and what you don't like) when you are sitting on the "student" end of the bench; make use of these insights as you prepare to sit at the "teacher" end.

What's Next

Whenever you present new information, it is important to give your students an overview of the material before you get into the gory details. Such an overview functions as a road map that tells learners where they are about to go, so they won't get lost along the way. Chapter Two, "A Blueprint for Computer Training," is your road map to this book. When you finish reading the chapter, you will be ready to absorb the details presented in the rest of the book.

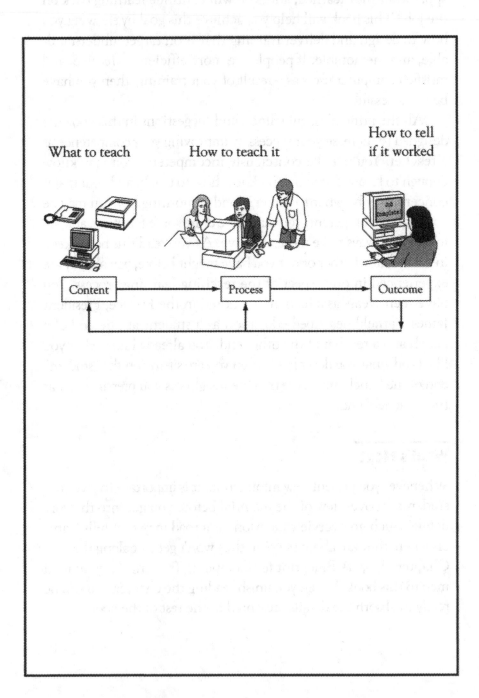

What to teach   How to teach it   How to tell if it worked

Content → Process → Outcome

2

A Blueprint for Computer Training

Report from the Trenches: Arming the Road Warriors

Drugz R Us is a pharmaceutical company with headquarters in Chicago and regional offices in Atlanta, Denver, Boston, and San Francisco. The company employs 327 sales reps, who visit physicians on a regular basis to spark interest in (and, it is hoped, increase sales of) the company's products. The best-selling product is Mindzap, a fast-acting antidepressant with no documented side effects.

Because the sales reps are on the road five days a week, it has been difficult for them to keep up with the company's stringent paperwork requirements. As a result, the president of Drugz R Us recently mandated that each rep will carry a notebook computer and complete the paperwork in his or her hotel room at night. The reps will use an application called Drugrunner, a vertical-market database program developed for the pharmaceutical industry and customized for Drugz R Us by their management information systems (MIS) department. Reps will be expected to update their individual Drugrunner database daily. Once a week, they will upload Drugrunner data to the regional office, where data from all of the reps in the region will be consolidated and sent to headquarters.

You are a systems analyst in the MIS department of Drugz R Us. When your department was asked to customize the Drugrunner program, you managed the project. And now, because you know Drugrunner better than anyone else, you have been asked to conduct training sessions for all 327 sales reps, to get them up to speed on the program. You were given only one imperative: make it snappy. Any time spent in the classroom is time away from the physicians' offices, and time is money.

Where do you start? "Hmmm," you murmur. "I guess I'd better plan on four training sessions: one in each region. And they said time is of the essence, so each session should last only a day. And maybe to speed things up I could design an on-line tutorial. . . ."

Nix. Stop. Halt. You're getting ahead of yourself. You have no idea what you need to teach, and you're already planning how to teach it! Until you figure out the content, you aren't ready to determine the process. So, take a deep breath, followed by one giant step backward.

Content: Figuring Out What to Teach

The first thing to realize is that you can't teach it all. Even if you had the time and the money (which, trust me, you don't), your learners would never sit still for it. Since you can't teach it all, you have to teach what's most important. Figuring out what's important also helps you figure out what's not important; in other words, what you choose to leave out of your training is as important as what you choose to leave in.

The process of defining what's important is called *needs assessment*. A trainer uses needs assessment the way a sculptor carves a tiger from a block of marble: by carefully using chisel and mallet to remove everything that isn't a tiger. What happens if you skip this critical first step? You may wind up with a beautiful statue of a duck. In other words, you may develop training that, while nicely designed, doesn't give learners the essential skills they will need to use a system.

To define what's important, your needs assessment should investigate three major variables: the *learners* you will be teaching, the *system* you will teach them to use, and the *work environment* in which these learners will be using the system (see Figure 2.1). Once you understand each of these variables, you can decide what to include in your training.

FIGURE 2.1. Three Major Variables of Needs Assessment.

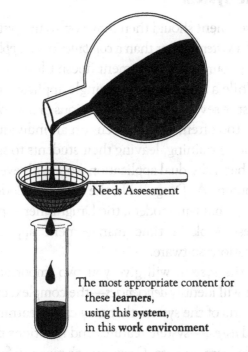

Needs Assessment

The most appropriate content for
these **learners,**
using this **system,**
in this **work environment**

Assessing the Learners

Your needs assessment should begin with the learners because what you teach depends partly on whom you are teaching. For instance, most of the Drugz R Us sales reps are in their mid twenties and used computers routinely in college. Since they are reasonably proficient in generic computer skills, your training will probably not have to include computer basics. Proficiency is one way to categorize learners; attitude is another. At Drugz R Us, the sales reps are split in their opinion of Drugrunner. Half of them are excited at the thought of getting notebook computers; the rest are furious that "Big Brother" will be encroaching on their private time.

Given these extreme views, you will need to decide whether to confront, cajole, or convince—or close your eyes and ignore the entire issue.

Assessing the System

Your needs assessment should then move on to the system. Thinking in terms of a *system* rather than a *computer* or an *application* helps you assure that your needs assessment doesn't leave out anything important. While a system may be a single application, it is more likely to consist of several related applications or a whole office full of machinery. Too often, trainers focus on an individual software application during training, leaving their students to struggle with how to make that individual application work with everything else on their computers. At Drugz R Us, the system includes the notebook computer, a built-in modem, the Drugrunner application, an on-line address book, a time management application, and telecommunications software.

Assessing the system will give you two important pieces of information: it will identify *deficiencies*—the complex, cumbersome, or confusing parts of the system that may cause learning problems for users—and *assets*—system features and functions that are particularly easy to learn and use. Drugrunner's major deficiency is the telecommunications software, which was developed by the modem manufacturer and requires long sequences of keystrokes that are inconsistent with all the other applications the reps will be using. The on-line address book, on the other hand, is so intuitive that it can be mastered in under ten minutes.

Assessing the Work Environment

Finally, your needs assessment should investigate the environment in which the learners will be using the system to do their jobs. Often, businesses make the fatal mistake of introducing new technology into work environments without considering the impact this technology will have on business processes. Whenever one aspect of a job changes, there is a ripple effect on all other aspects of the job. Also, some work environments are more able than others to absorb technological changes. Some already have mechanisms in place to support new users, such as help desks, on-the-job training, or resident gurus. Work environments that lack such mechanisms impose a greater burden on trainers; once students go back to their jobs, they are essentially on their own. At Drugz R Us, the work environment is really 327 little work environments, each consisting of the sales rep, the rep's current hotel room, and several hundred physicians' offices. Plunked into this environment will be Drugrunner and its accompanying paraphernalia.

Process: Planning How to Teach the Content

After you have investigated the people, the system, and the work environment to determine *what* you need to teach, you are ready to plan *how* to teach it. Your goal is to be both *efficient* and *effective:* to present the most appropriate information in the least amount of time, and to do it in such a way that your students remember what you told them long after you leave. This, like most principles, is easy to articulate but difficult to accomplish. A grasshopper once went to the wise old owl with a complaint: every winter he ran out of food and developed frostbite. "No problem," said the bird. "Crickets hibernate during the winter months. Become a cricket, and you will no longer suffer." "But I'm a grasshopper! How can I become a cricket?" cried the desperate insect. And the owl replied: "Hey! I gave you the basic principle. It's up to you to figure out the implementation."

Instructional Methods

To be an efficient and effective trainer, you need to understand how adults learn and which instructional methods are best suited to teaching computer skills. Fortunately, we know considerably more about this than we do about morphing grasshoppers into crickets! A great deal of research has been done in the fields of cognitive science and instructional design. Cognitive scientists investigate how the brain works; instructional designers translate these general principles of cognition into practical techniques.

The principles of cognitive science and instructional design are applicable to any subject matter, from astrophysics to Nordic mythology. Teaching people to use computers poses an additional challenge: a computer system is much more than the monitor, the keyboard, or even what users see on the screen. These are the visible parts of a system. Much of what goes on when people interact with computers is invisible. A user types the command PRINT or clicks on a picture of a printer, and—lo and behold—out pops a hard copy of the annual report—or it doesn't, as the case may be. If the report prints, the user will probably attempt the same sequence of actions the next time he or she wants to print something. If the report doesn't print, the user has to figure out why it didn't and what to do about it. Was PRINT the wrong command to use in this case? Is the printer out of paper? Is there a bug in the software?

We humans are always trying to fathom the meaning or nature of the world around us. We need to find reasons why something happens—especially when something goes wrong. So, if a user presses a key and the printer beeps twice and dies, that user will come up with a theory of why it happened. Sometimes it's the correct theory—frequently it's the wrong one. In either case, it's the user's attempt to make sense of the environment.

These ways of making sense of the environment are called *mental models*. When people learn to use computers, mental models explain the relationship between their actions and the system's response. Mental models link the visible parts and processes of a system with its invisible parts and processes (see Figure 2.2). For instance, the Upload Data icon in the Drugrunner database is a visible part of the system. All the system actions that go on behind the scenes after the sales rep selects this icon are invisible processes.

FIGURE 2.2. Linking the Visible to the Invisible with Mental Models.

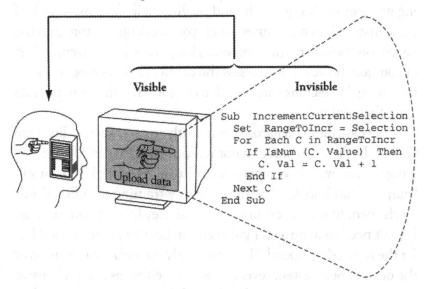

Since you can't teach it all, mental models are an important way for learners to correctly interpret new situations that were not addressed during training. Efficient and effective computer training helps people build mental models that will guide them once they are back on the job, far from your benign gaze.

Instructional Materials

Speaking of that benign gaze: what happens after training is finished and you and your students go your separate ways? As you plan computer training, it can be tempting to focus exclusively on what will happen when you and your students interact. But remember: you won't always be interacting. Your ultimate goal is to help people become independent. Although training is necessary to meet this goal, it is not sufficient. You also need to provide support materials. There are many kinds of support materials, and various ones are appropriate under various circumstances. Selecting the right ones, and designing your own when none exist, is an essential part of the teaching-learning process.

Three common types of materials that support computer training are user guides, job aids, and on-line help systems. Think of these materials as parachutes: when your students venture into the system on their own, these materials keep them from crashing. Part of your job, however, is to assess the quality of these support materials, as real parachutes are tested, to be sure that they will truly do what they claim.

The Drugrunner database comes with an extensive on-line help system. In fact, this was a major reason why Drugz R Us selected Drugrunner over its competitors. "Great," you think to yourself, "maybe I can knock a few hours off the training session. I'll just teach them to use the on-line help, and they'll be off and running. I won't need to write a user guide either. Less for me to do, and less for the reps to lug around." Unfortunately, a careful examination of the on-line help system reveals that it is neither as comprehensive nor as easy to use as the vendor claimed. It contains some basic data entry rules, and a good index of technical terms, but it provides no step-by-step instructions for Drugrunner procedures. Your challenge will be to weave the assets of the on-line help system into your training and support materials, while anticipating and supplementing its deficiencies.

Outcome: Discovering Whether They Got It

Cinderella had two ugly stepsisters; training has only one. Her name is "Outcome." Outcome is what keeps you honest: it asks the basic question, "How well did this training work?" Outcome is one of those concepts that everyone agrees is essential, and nobody wants to tackle. For one thing, it is hard to measure. For another, what if the answer turns out to be, "As a matter of fact, the training didn't work particularly well"? Hopefully, that will never happen to you. Hopefully, your training will have a positive impact on the people you train and, ultimately, on the entire organization. However, if you want credit for your success, you will have to demonstrate that you were successful.

For most trainers, even "accidental trainers," teaching people to use computers is not a one-shot deal. If you have been asked to teach once, you will be asked to teach again. Every teaching experience can be an opportunity for you to improve. This means you need to know what worked, so you can do more of it, and what didn't work, so you can fix it. Suppose you fly out to the San Francisco region, train the 78 Drugz R Us sales reps on Drugrunner, send them on their way, and simply hope for the best. One month later, you are summoned to the president's office. The San Francisco reps are making horrendous data entry errors, and every time they upload their data to headquarters, the programmers have to work overtime to repair the corporate database. Organizational costs are going up due to the massive amounts of rework time. The president is not happy. You are not happy. Chances are the training is at least partly to blame. But what aspect(s) of the training caused the errors? It could be a *content* problem: although you did a good job of teaching, you taught the wrong information. In other words, you missed something during needs assessment. Or it could be a *process* problem: you taught the right information but you either taught it poorly or you provided inadequate support materials for reps to use after training. One thing is for sure: you'd better find out quickly, before you teach the Denver, Atlanta, and Boston courses.

There are two ways to evaluate training outcomes: you can evaluate teaching, and you can evaluate learning. I often ask trainers this deceptively simple question: If the learner didn't learn, did the teacher teach? Some trainers tell me that if they have presented information well, they are effective teachers even if their students did not absorb the material. Other trainers believe that while they may have been doing something at the front of the classroom that looked remarkably like teaching, unless their students were learning, they were not teaching. There is no right or wrong answer to this question, because teaching and learning are intertwined. Nevertheless, it is useful to think of them separately when evaluating training outcomes.

Evaluating Teaching

First, you can look at teaching. You can use a combination of questionnaires and interviews to find out how your students perceived the training. Learners can give you valuable information about how they experienced the training, including feedback on what you taught and how you taught it. Administering a one-page attitude survey to the Drugz R Us sales reps might uncover the fact that most reps found your delivery too fast-paced, with too much jargon and too few examples. You can also ask a colleague or a more experienced trainer to review your lesson plans or observe your teaching. Since training is a lonely business, feedback from another trainer can help you figure out if you are on track. If an experienced trainer had looked at your Drugrunner course materials before the San Francisco course, she might have recommended that you develop a "cheat sheet" to remind the sales reps of the confusing data entry codes. She also might have noticed that all your exercises had the sales reps working in pairs. Since the reps will be working on Drugrunner alone after training is over, she might have suggested that the learners should complete some of these exercises independently.

Evaluating Learning

While it is important to evaluate teaching, ultimately the goal of training is *learning*. That is, students should be able to do more after training than they could before. There is really only one way to evaluate learning: with formal or informal testing. It is sometimes appropriate to administer a written test at the end of a course. Often, however, the most valuable way to evaluate learning is by observing students during hands-on exercises. You might create a simulation where each sales rep is given a different set of weekly sales figures and is told to follow all the steps necessary to enter these figures into the computer, check the figures for accuracy, and upload the data to the main computer. It is no coincidence that these are exactly the skills the reps will need on the job. By observing them as they complete the simulation, you will get a good indication of how well they mastered Drugrunner.

What's Next

Section One has acknowledged the challenges that you face as a computer trainer. It has also introduced you to the notion of content, process, and outcome (see Figure 2.3)—the blueprint for computer training that is expanded upon in the remaining sections of the book. The chapters in these sections give you ways to define the content, process, and outcome of your training. They help you to answer these three questions:

What should I teach? (Section Two)

How should I teach it? (Section Three)

How can I tell if it worked? (Section Four)

Section Two discusses the first of the three questions. It focuses on content: how to make sure you teach what's important, since you can't teach it all. The three chapters in this section describe methods for assessing the learner (Chapter Three), the system (Chapter Four), and the work environment (Chapter Five) to ensure that your training is on target.

FIGURE 2.3. A Blueprint for Computer Training.

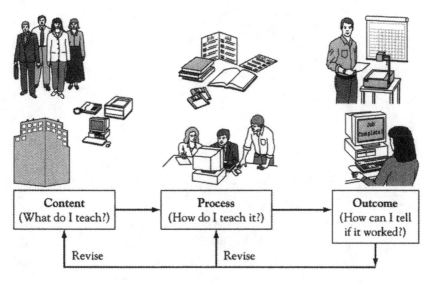

SECTION TWO

What Should I Teach?

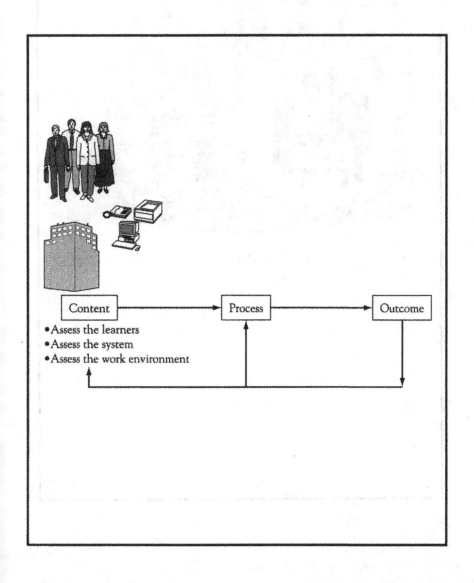

3

Assessing the Learners

Know Your Audience

**Report from the Trenches:
What's Wrong with This Picture?**

Safe Entertainment Enterprises (SEE) is a Utah-based cable television company that specializes in family-oriented programming. The company has expanded rapidly over the past two years, opening regional offices in Wyoming, Montana, Idaho, and New Mexico. Nine months ago they hired an outside vendor to develop a major upgrade to their existing customer billing system. Tacked onto the end of the contract, almost as an afterthought, was a commitment from the vendor to train the clerical staff who would use the system.

Amazingly, the upgrade was delivered on time and within budget. In accordance with the contract, one of the vendor's trainers has arrived at SEE headquarters in Salt Lake City to teach the data entry clerks how to operate the new system. The first group of trainees files into the classroom and sits patiently as the trainer sets up her overhead projector and the LCD panel that projects an enlarged image of the computer system. The lights are dimmed. The first image appears. "This is called a *computer screen,*" chirps the trainer. "It's just like a paper form, only instead of filling in the blanks by hand, you type on a *keyboard,* which is a lot like a typewriter. How many of you have used a typewriter before?" There is dead silence as the trainees—whizbang computer operators who have used the old billing system for an average of three years—exchange glances. Someone suppresses a giggle; several others sigh. As the silence lengthens, the trainer frowns; she can't understand what's going wrong. The last time she ran this course, the students loved it. What's the matter with this group?

Why Assess the Learners?

You have to know whom you are teaching before you can decide what to teach them. While this sounds like common sense, the sad fact is that trainers often make incorrect assumptions about the skills of their learners—and don't discover their error until it's too late. A widespread complaint of participants in computer training classes is that the instruction is either over their heads or under their feet. When trainers skip the critical first step of learner assessment, they run the risk of creating training that either underestimates or overestimates the abilities of their students.

The challenge is that learners come in many different flavors. They differ in their abilities, their past experiences, and their attitudes. What works for one type of learner may be a resounding failure with another. This chapter gives you some ways of thinking about these learner differences so you can visualize your audience as you plan the content of your training.

Learners Differ in Proficiency

One way to differentiate learners is by proficiency—that is, to determine how much learners know about systems in general and about their system in particular. There has been a dramatic fluctuation in the proficiency of computer users over the last fifty years. In the 1950s and 1960s, most people who used computers were technically skilled: they were primarily programmers, engineers, and others of their ilk. These highly sophisticated users often mastered this new technology on their own. Any formal training they received simply added to their extensive store of knowledge. A major shift occurred in the 1970s and 1980s with the proliferation of technology in all parts of the workplace. Suddenly, large numbers of technologically unskilled office workers had to conquer complex computer systems. For these beginners, training needed to do more than present the steps required to run an application; it had to teach a whole new way of thinking. Now that the end of the century is nearly upon us, the "Nintendo generation" has started to enter the workforce. This has led to yet another proficiency shift: users who are computer conversant. Neither sophisticates nor beginners, these people, on the one hand, know what it is like to interact with a computer, and they do not find these interactions threatening. On the other hand, their range of experience is typically limited, and training is necessary to bring them up to speed on the systems they must interact with to do their jobs.

The purpose of this romp through history is to help you resist using the terms "novice" and "expert" when you assess the proficiency of your learners. Rarely will you find a learner who fits neatly into either category; most learners are somewhere along a continuum (see Figure 3.1).[1] These days, most people have at least been exposed to a computer. There are computers in the library, the bank, the video rental store, and on fellow workers' desks. In that sense, you will rarely see a "novice" learner. Conversely, any learner might be considered a "novice" in the sense that he or she is unfamiliar with the information you are about to teach. So, either nobody is a novice, or everyone is, which makes this a less-than-useful way to describe learners. By the same token, the term "expert" carries with it the implication that no further learning is possible, whereas the truth is that when people interact with computers, learning never stops; even long-time users are continually refining and sharpening their skills.

Let's examine the characteristics of learners along the proficiency continuum.

FIGURE 3.1. The Proficiency Continuum.

Naive ──────────────────────────────────────► Experienced

Source: Weiss, E. *Making Computers People-Literate*. San Francisco: Jossey-Bass, 1994.

Naive Users Are System Aware

At the lowest end of the continuum is the naive user. The *American Heritage* dictionary defines naive as "lacking critical ability or analytical insight." These users are naive because their exposure to computers has been limited. They may tell you things like: "I'm hopeless—a rank beginner—totally computer illiterate!" Yet, if you probe further, you will discover that they understand more than they think they do. While they may lack analytic insight, they are not clueless! Perhaps they routinely use an ATM machine to make bank deposits, or their teenager uses a computer to complete school assignments. They may even (albeit timidly) use the company's E-mail system to communicate with colleagues. In other words, although naive, these users are *system aware*.

For example, Gloria Sanchez is a graphic artist for a large ad agency. She also does volunteer work for her city's homeless shelter. As part of the shelter's annual fund-raising campaign, she has offered to design and mail a brochure to five hundred prior donors. A colleague has suggested that one of the ad agency's computers could be used to generate mailing labels for the brochures, and he has offered to teach Gloria how to set up the donor names and addresses in a database. Gloria's experience with computers has been minimal. For the past three years, she has used the word processing software on her son's home computer to write her annual Christmas letter (although she lets him do the formatting). She has also watched her daughter, an accounting major at the local business college, use a money management program to track the family finances. Gloria is a little nervous, but she is sure she can learn to use the database—as long as someone shows her what to do every step of the way.

System-Savvy Users Have Breadth

Let's assume that Gloria masters the database program and returns in triumph to the homeless shelter with a stack of mailing labels. Let's take it one step further: made bold by her success, she lets her daughter teach her how to use the money management program. Then, she sneaks a peek at the word processor's user manual and learns to format her own Christmas letters. Gloria has moved up the proficiency continuum, from system aware to *system savvy*.

System-savvy users have a practical understanding of what computers are and how they work. They either have used several different types of applications (for example, a word processor, a spreadsheet, and an E-mail program) and understand the similarities and differences among them, or they have used only one type of application, such as graphics software, but have used several different graphics programs, each of which has different commands, functions, and procedures. The key characteristic of system-savvy users is *breadth*. They don't know a whole lot about each system they have used, but they understand the basics of all of them. Because they have interacted with a variety of systems, they have started to develop a mental model that explains how computers work. They have learned how to learn about computers.

Task-Savvy Users Have Perspective

Gloria can be considered system savvy because she has learned a bit about three diverse types of systems: databases, financial managers, and word processors. Now let's give her a new challenge. Guess what her ad agency decides to do? That's right: each graphic artist is issued a brand new, state-of-the-art computer and told that within six months it must be used for all assignments. The agency has hired a trainer to bring the artists up to speed on the new system, and is willing to send them to additional seminars as needed, but any artists who feel they can't make the transition from sketch pad to screen are invited to look elsewhere for jobs.

It is fortunate for Gloria that she is already system savvy, which just goes to show the benefits of doing volunteer work. But Gloria has another advantage: she is also *task savvy*. That is, she already knows how to do the work—she has simply never done it on a computer.

Users who are both system savvy and task savvy are higher on the proficiency continuum than users who are simply system savvy. The key characteristic of task-savvy users is *perspective*. Because task-savvy users are skilled practitioners, their learning challenge is primarily to figure out how to do what they already know they need to do. For example, Gloria is a skilled designer. She already knows that Pantone 313, 328, and 512 are the best match of colors to communicate a particular advertising message. During training, she can focus her energy on the procedures required to select these colors on the computer.

Syntax-Savvy Users Have Depth

At the highest end of the proficiency continuum is the experienced user. The *American Heritage* dictionary defines experienced as "skilled or knowledgeable as the result of active participation or practice." Experienced users are *syntax savvy:* they have mastered the rules necessary to operate a specific system. For example, Gloria has learned that color selection is accomplished by double-clicking on an object, pulling down the `Object` menu, and selecting the `Fill` command. If the agency had purchased a different graphics program, the same task might be accomplished by typing the coordinates of the object and then typing the appropriate Pantone code. Although the task is identical, the rules of syntax required to accomplish the task will vary from system to system. While system-savvy users have breadth, and task-savvy users have perspective, the key characteristic of syntax-savvy users is *depth*. Because of their active participation in the system, these users have mastered its rules of grammar, and the more time they spend with the system, the more experienced they become.

So there you have it: the range of learner proficiency from naive user to experienced user. Every student you teach will fall somewhere along this continuum. In fact, if you teach groups, chances are excellent that the entire continuum will be represented in a single class! In order to decide what to teach, you will need to know whether your learners are naive, experienced, or somewhere in between. Techniques for determining learner proficiency are discussed later in this chapter, and Chapter Six addresses the often confounding problem of handling classes in which learners are at different proficiency levels. But first, let's look at another way to differentiate learners: by attitude.

Learners Differ in Attitude

Every student you will ever teach enters the training situation with an attitude. The attitude may be enthusiastic or hostile, timid or confident, cautiously optimistic or optimistically cautious, or a combination of any of these. In some cases, the student's attitude will change as a result of the training. In other cases, the student will leave the training having the same attitude with which he or she entered it—which is either good news or bad news for the trainer.

Students come to training with attitudes about several things. They have feelings about the system itself, feelings about how the system will affect their job, and feelings about attending training. You may or may not be able to do anything to change these attitudes— and it may not even be wise to try. However, if you are aware of how your learners are feeling, you may be able to use this information to shape the content of your training. At the very least, forewarned is forearmed!

Learners Have Attitudes About Computers

The first attitude you need to consider is how learners feel about computers in general, and about the particular system you are teaching them to use. The important thing to remember here is that perception is reality. On the one hand, a system may be complex and time-consuming to learn; but if everyone in the office believes that it's the greatest innovation since Casual Fridays, you probably won't encounter hostile stares when the training begins. On the other hand, a system may be carefully designed and well-suited to the needs of the organization; but if common wisdom says that the system is a dog, you will have to struggle to convince learners otherwise.

Learners Have Attitudes About the System's Impact on Their Work

Learners will also have attitudes about the system's impact on their work. Whenever technology is introduced into an organization, there is a ripple effect across all jobs and work processes. Some systems are universally advantageous: they let everyone get more done in less time and with less effort. Other systems may help some parts of the organization while demanding extra energy from others. For instance, a group of middle managers may be delighted that their department has purchased a system that streamlines the process of generating quarterly financial reports. If they currently spend fifteen hours a month on these reports and the system lets them accomplish the same task in three hours, they will be eager for training. However, suppose these same middle managers were never expected to generate quarterly financial reports in the past. Perhaps these reports have traditionally been prepared by the company's MIS department and simply distributed to the middle managers. While the introduction of the new system will save time for the MIS department, it will add to the middle managers' workload. In this case, the middle managers may be less than enthusiastic about learning to use the system.

Learners Have Attitudes About Training

You can further assume that learners will have attitudes about attending training. Most adult learners approach training with what is commonly called the "WIIFM" question—What's in it for me?—and they will expect you to provide the answer. Adults have busy schedules; whether the training is a formal class or a one-on-one tutoring session, time spent in training means time away from either work or family. This conflict may lead to some ambivalence. Busy office managers who have been sent to a public seminar on advanced word processing techniques may be eager to master the software, yet they may find it difficult to ignore thoughts of the three-foot-high stack of phone messages that will await them after two days away from the office. Conversely, learner attitudes are often positive if training is perceived as a reward. The secretary who has recently been promoted to office manager may be eager to learn the advanced word processing skills that she will need for her new job. Even if training is viewed as personally beneficial, however, there may still be some ambivalence. The same secretary may be worried about her ability to master the complexities of the software, and she may feel concerned that she is in over her head.

Uncovering Learner Proficiency and Attitude

So far, this chapter has examined two ways that learners can differ: in proficiency and in attitude. You've learned that all learners fall somewhere along a continuum from naive to experienced, and that everyone you teach will have preexisting attitudes about the system, the system's impact on their work, and the training itself. Unless you find out about your learners beforehand, you run the risk of conducting training that is either too basic or too advanced, and that does not take into account the essential concerns of your students. Remember the SEE cable company case at the beginning of this chapter? When last we saw the trainer, she was standing in front of an unresponsive group of data entry clerks, scratching her head and wondering what was wrong with them. Had she done a little homework before she flew to Salt Lake City, here is what she would have discovered about the learners:

1.   *None of these data entry clerks are naive users.* Seventy percent are high on the proficiency continuum: they are both system savvy (familiar with computers) and task savvy (they have been doing customer billing at SEE for an average of three years). They are also syntax savvy on the old billing system (they know all the commands and procedures necessary to operate it). The remaining thirty percent of the students are new hires. They all have data entry experience from prior jobs, but they have not worked in customer billing before and are new to the cable industry. This makes them system savvy, but not task savvy. As a result, they are lower on the proficiency continuum.

2.   *Attitudes toward the new billing system, and toward the impact the system will have on their jobs, are mixed.* The clerks all agree that the old system had serious flaws: it used arcane data entry codes that were difficult to learn and easy to forget; it required them to jump through hoops whenever they had to correct errors; and it always seemed to break down in the middle of printing billing statements. The clerks are not sorry to see the last of the old system. Nevertheless, they have spent the past twelve months watching the vendor's programmers sit in a little room writing code to upgrade the system—and never once have these programmers asked them for their opinions about how to make the system better. Not only are the data entry clerks insulted, they are worried. They aren't sure that these programmers understood the cable business well enough to design a system that will make their jobs easier. They have come to training with a "wait and see" attitude—and they are prepared to wait.

3.   *Attitudes toward the training are positive.* SEE does not have a tradition of providing formal training to its employees; when new personnel are hired, they are generally teamed up with experienced employees and told to observe until they can do the work on their own. Sometimes this on-the-job training approach is successful, but

often the new people spend weeks floundering until they get the hang of the job. Providing classroom training on the new billing system represents a radical change for the company. The data entry clerks see this as an important step in the right direction and are rooting for its success.

Could the trainer have uncovered these three learner characteristics before conducting the training? You bet. After all, there was plenty of time: the upgrade was in development for nine months. The trainer could have arranged for the data entry clerks to complete a simple proficiency survey, like the one shown in Exhibit 3.1. The results of this survey would have cued her that she could begin the training session at a more advanced level. She could have interviewed a few of the data entry clerks to find out how they felt about the old system and how they anticipated feeling about the new one. This would have alerted her to the students' concerns about the impact of the new system on their jobs, which she could have addressed right at the start of the training session. Finally, if she or someone else from her company had talked to SEE senior management, they would have uncovered the crucial fact that a lot was riding on the success of this particular training program.

Sometimes, of course, it simply isn't possible to gather data about learners before training starts. Trainers who run public seminars on popular software applications, for example, never know who will walk through the door until that door actually opens. Neither do trainers who conduct one-on-one informal training sessions as the need arises; they may not know until five minutes ahead of time that they are going to be training someone. If either of these describes your situation, you will need to become adept at "learner assessment on the fly." This means tuning into all the verbal and nonverbal messages that your learners send out. Above all, you need to be flexible: ready to change your focus at a moment's notice, if necessary. If you are running a course on advanced page-layout techniques and you realize that half the students are staring blankly at you when you tell them to set up a master page with two columns

EXHIBIT 3.1. Sample Survey to Determine Learner Proficiency.

1	How long have you worked on the current billing system?	☐ Not at all ☐ Days or weeks ☐ Several months ☐ A year or more
2	How much time do you spend per week using the current billing system?	☐ None ☐ 1–5 hours ☐ 6–15 hours ☐ More than 15 hours
3	How many other systems have you worked with?	☐ None ☐ 1–3 ☐ 4 or more
4	How would you rate your general level of computer expertise?	☐ I'm just learning to use computers ☐ I can use computers to do my work ☐ I can help others use computers
5	How familiar are you with the job of customer billing?	☐ I really don't know much about this job ☐ I have been doing this job for some time ☐ I have taught others to do this job

and a centered page number, while the remaining students are merrily proceeding to carry out your instructions, you had better be willing to make a quick change to your course design—or you will have wasted everyone's time and money. If you are helping a coworker master the company's E-mail system and he acts fidgety when you slowly and carefully explain how a modem works, a few well-placed questions may tell you that he used E-mail extensively in his last job and simply needs instructions on the specific commands required to use this system.

What's Next

This chapter has addressed the importance of finding out about your learners. Remember, though, that these learners do not operate in a vacuum. They are surrounded by both the computer system you are teaching them to use and the work environment in which they will be using it. Chapter Four tackles the second of these elements: the thorny problem of system usability. In other words, what are the strengths and weaknesses of this particular system? How do you identify those strengths and weaknesses so that you can target your training to the parts of the system that may cause problems for learners?

4

Assessing the Usability of the System

Know Your Challenges

Report from the Trenches: Oh, Balderdash!

Balderdash Books is a discount book chain with a rapidly expanding retail presence throughout the United States. Founded in 1961 by the little-known Beat poet Sidney Balderdash, the company enjoyed modest success in upstate New York for three decades. In 1993, Sidney's son Kerouac took over as president and began an aggressive expansion effort. Balderdash now has seventy-two stores in thirty major cities, and plans to triple this figure over the next two years. The company is about to scrap its outdated warehousing system and replace it with PictoTrack, an inventory management system developed in-house by the Balderdash MIS department. PictoTrack is designed to support the company's warehouse in Buffalo, New York.

Rodney is Balderdash's vice president of operations. He is excited about upgrading the warehouse to PictoTrack. Ever since the company's growth spurt, inventory management has been a colossal headache for Operations. Rodney has been assured by Felicia, the MIS director, that the system's graphical user interface (GUI) and on-line help system will virtually eliminate the need for end-user training and documentation, and that warehouse personnel will be able to learn the system in a matter of hours.

Felicia is also excited about PictoTrack. This is the first system her MIS department has built that uses the GUI approach. A graphic artist was brought in to consult on icon design and color selection, and Felicia is delighted with the results. She harbors a secret hope that after PictoTrack is successfully installed at Balderdash, her department will be able to market the system to other discount booksellers.

Tomàs is excited about PictoTrack, too. He is the Balderdash training manager. Budget cuts have left him with only three end-user trainers to support all the automated systems at Balderdash. These trainers are also responsible for course development, so the budget cuts have dramatically reduced the number of hours each trainer can spend in the classroom. Consequently, the prospect of a system that people can learn in a few hours is tremendously appealing.

Paul is one of those end-user trainers. He isn't excited about much of anything. Paul has just received a memo from Tomàs informing him that Paul will be responsible for PictoTrack training and documentation. The memo contains a strong hint that Rodney, the client, wants a short course, and an even shorter user guide. Paul has never even seen a demonstration of PictoTrack, but he is hoping desperately that it's as good as everyone has promised.

Why Is Usability Important?

When people interact with computer systems to get a job done, the interaction can range from pleasant to neutral to exceedingly painful. Where a particular system falls on this continuum is largely determined by its *user interface*. The user interface is the part of a system with which users interact directly; it might include the placement of information on a screen, the commands a user types to complete a task, the method for getting from one screen to another, and the error messages displayed when the user makes a mistake.

Every computer system has a user interface. In fact, every piece of equipment with which we interact can be said to have a user interface of one sort or another. Take a look at your telephone.

There's no screen, but you do interact with it: you lift up the handset to indicate that you want to make a call, you push buttons to activate the call, and you hang up the handset to end the call. If you have a fancy phone system in your office, there may be buttons you can push for other tasks, such as conferencing, paging, transferring, and the like. While a system with a well-designed user interface is a joy and a delight, a system with a poorly designed user interface can lead to the following problems for users and their organizations:[1]

- It takes people too long to learn to use the system.
- Over time, people forget what they learned during training.
- Too much effort is required for people to complete tasks.
- People make too many errors when they use the system.
- When people use the system they feel frustrated, angry, or inept.

Ideally, every system should have a well-designed user interface. In the real world, however, all systems have at least some design flaws. Sometimes these flaws are due to an unclear understanding of user needs ("I'll go talk to the users and find out what they want. The rest of you start writing code"). Sometimes they are due to cost considerations ("We don't have the budget to make it pretty; we'll let the trainers and tech writers pitch it to the users after we're done"), and sometimes to insufficient usability testing ("We're already behind schedule on this; let's just get Release 1.0 out there in the marketplace and improve it later").

Why Assess Usability If You Can't Fix the System?

The best time to conduct a usability assessment is while a system is in development. The goal is to learn what works and what doesn't, to uncover any parts of the interface that don't work smoothly for users. Since at this stage the system is still fairly fluid, the user interface can be redesigned to make it easier to use.

As a computer trainer, however, you generally work with systems that have already been built. Whether the systems are commercial software packages or large in-house applications, you don't have the luxury of improving them; you simply have to make the best of whatever you've been given. So, why assess a system's usability if you can't fix the system? You assess a system for the same reason you assess your learners: to determine the content of your training. Chapter Three discussed the fact that learners vary by proficiency and by attitude. It explored how assessing these two dimensions helps you to decide what (and how much) to teach. Unless you know how savvy your students are about computers, you run the risk of either overwhelming or boring them. Unless you know how your students feel about systems in general, and this system in particular, your training may fail to address crucial concerns.

When you assess the usability of a system, your goal is to uncover its strengths and weaknesses so that your training can accommodate them. During usability assessment, you discover which parts of the user interface are likely to support your learners: perhaps the system has an on-line help facility that explains each choice on its menus, or perhaps color is used effectively to remind users to save their work. You also discover which parts of the user interface are most likely to cause problems for your learners: perhaps the system requires users to memorize complex data entry codes, or perhaps the method for correcting errors is confusing and time-consuming. Once you find these weaknesses, you can make sure you address them during training. The rest of this chapter describes a simple and effective way to assess the usability of a system.

The Four Faces of a User Interface

This chapter has already noted that the user interface lets a person interact with the system. Few user interfaces are all good or all bad— each interface has elements that work well and other elements that don't. To sort out these elements, you need a precise and structured way to describe what you see. I find it helpful to think of the user interface as a four-faced creature (see Figure 4.1), with each "face" representing a distinct set of interactions.[2] For example, when you look at information on a screen, you are interacting with the *presentation* interface. When you type a command, you are interacting with the *conversation* interface. When you select a menu choice to get to a different part of the system, you are interacting with the *navigation* interface. And when you ask for on-line help, you are interacting with the *explanation* interface.

1. *The presentation interface* controls how users are shown information. It includes the elements of screen design, graphics, and color.
   Example: All data entry fields are colored blue to make them easy to see. Error messages are displayed in red to indicate their importance. Icons representing frequent user commands are displayed in a row across the bottom of the screen.

2. *The conversation interface* controls how the system and the user "talk" to each other. It includes the elements of user-to-system communication, such as commands, and system-to-user communication, such as system prompts.

FIGURE 4.1. The Four Faces of Human-Computer Interaction.

Example: On a sales order screen, users can either type a product code in the appropriate data entry field or select the correct code from a pop-up list. When users complete the screen, the system displays a message indicating that the order is ready to be shipped.

3. *The navigation interface* controls how users make their way from one part of the system to another. It includes methods such as menus, direct manipulation, and keystrokes for moving within a screen and from screen to screen.

Example: Users move from one screen to another by clicking on graphical icons that represent system functions. To get to the screen for entering a sales order, they click on a picture of a pencil. To get to the screen that uploads the order to the warehouse, they click on a picture of a telephone. To get to the dialogue box that prints a hard copy of the order, they click on a picture of a printer.

4. *The explanation interface* controls the way the system teaches users about itself. It includes the elements of error handling and on-line help.

Example: When users make a mistake, the system displays a brief error message. Experienced users can correct the mistake immediately. New users can press a special <HELP> key to get more instructions on the nature of the mistake, why it happened, and how they can fix it.

Categorizing a system's user interface into these four components makes it easier to examine it for usability. How often have you sat down to learn a new software application only to get up a few hours later with vague feelings of frustration but no way to articulate just what it was about the system that didn't work for you? You might have used adjectives like "hard," "clunky," or "hostile" (or perhaps some other adjectives unsuitable for a family publication). If you want to ensure that you are teaching what is most important, you will need a greater degree of precision in evaluating a system's user interface. Let's examine each of the four components in more detail.

Assessing the Presentation Interface

The presentation interface is a system's public face. When a system's presentation interface is well-designed, it is both familiar and transparent. A *familiar* interface uses metaphors to present system concepts, terms, and tasks. As you may remember from seventh-grade English, metaphors relate two otherwise unrelated things; if learners are familiar with one thing, they will find it easier to understand the other. For example, a common metaphor uses the language of manual filing systems to describe computer data structures. Thus, users are shown "file cabinets" (not libraries), "folders" (not directories), and "documents" (not data files).

While a familiar interface helps users make the transition from the technical to the known, a *transparent* interface protects users from the technical. Just as drivers needn't know how an internal combustion engine works to get from one end of town to the other, so computer users shouldn't have to know the inner workings of a spreadsheet program to calculate an annual budget. For example, to edit a formula in a spreadsheet, users double-click on the cell containing the formula and make their changes, then press the <RETURN> key to save their changes or the <ESCAPE> key to restore the original formula. These three simple actions may require the spreadsheet program to do hundreds of behind-the-scenes somersaults that the user knows nothing about.

Exhibit 4.1 provides a sample checklist that can be used to evaluate a system's presentation interface. After you rank each item, you will know whether this aspect of the system is likely to cause learning problems for users. Since the presentation interface is the first thing users see when they "meet" a new system, poor design in this area can affect user perceptions of the rest of the system. Any design flaws you find are good candidates to include in your training.

EXHIBIT 4.1. Usability Assessment Checklist: Presentation Interface.

#	What to Look for	Always	Sometimes	Never	N/A
1	Visual cues and white space are used to create symmetry, to lead the eye in the appropriate direction, and to distinguish among different screen objects.	☐	☐	☐	☐
2	All data a user needs to complete a system task are on display at all times, from the start of the task until the end.	☐	☐	☐	☐
3	System messages are visually distinct and consistently appear where the user is likely to be looking on the screen.	☐	☐	☐	☐
4	For GUI (graphical user interface) systems, the icons that represent system objects and procedures are concrete, familiar, and conceptually distinct.	☐	☐	☐	☐
5	For GUI systems that use multiple windows, it is easy for users to enlarge, reduce, and rearrange windows.	☐	☐	☐	☐
6	If users select system functions from menus, the choices on these menus are consistently ordered in a way that is logical and easy to remember.	☐	☐	☐	☐
7	Color is used consistently and appropriately to communicate meaningful information to users.	☐	☐	☐	☐

Assessing the Conversation Interface

The conversation interface is a system's personality. Two character-istics of a well-designed conversation interface are clear dialogue and effective feedback. *Clear dialogue* makes it easy for a system's users to send information to the system and to interpret the infor-mation that the system sends back to them. For example, users should be able to type "quit," "end," or "exit" (*not* "kill" or "termi-nate") to close an application. The system should display the message Out of paper. Add paper and type Y to continue, or N to stop printing rather than ERROR34X2: Run aborted.

A system with timely and understandable *feedback* lets users know the consequences (positive or negative) of their actions. If you have ever had the experience of invoking a computer command and wondering if the system "heard" you, then you know the importance of feedback. For example, after the user issues the command to save a document, the system might display the message Work saved. It might highlight an icon after the user clicks on it to indicate that the icon has indeed been selected. It might display the message Processing . . . during a lengthy system operation, to let the user know that something is happening behind the scenes.

Exhibit 4.2 provides a sample checklist that can be used to eval-uate a system's conversation interface. After you rank each item, you will know whether this aspect of the system is likely to cause learning problems for users. Systems with laborious system-to-user and user-to-system communications are typically time-consuming to master and difficult to use. If you find problems, you must be pre-pared to address them in your training.

Assessing the Navigation Interface

If the presentation interface is a system's public face and the con-versation interface is its personality, you can think of the navigation interface as its circulatory system. A well-designed navigation inter-face has visibility and provides shortcuts. A system with *visibility* lets

EXHIBIT 4.2. Usability Assessment Checklist:
Conversation Interface.

#	What to Look for	Always	Sometimes	Never	N/A
1	The system uses terminology that can be readily understood by users.	☐	☐	☐	☐
2	System messages are unambiguous, nonthreatening, and informative.	☐	☐	☐	☐
3	There is system feedback for every user action.	☐	☐	☐	☐
4	The user is kept informed about all actions the system is taking.	☐	☐	☐	☐
5	The names of menus and menu choices are understandable and mutually exclusive.	☐	☐	☐	☐
6	If users communicate with the system via a command language, these commands are easy to learn and remember.	☐	☐	☐	☐
7	If users communicate with the system via a graphical user interface (GUI), the purpose of each graphic object is immediately apparent and unambiguous.	☐	☐	☐	☐

users see all available options at all times. For example, in an E-mail application, icons that represent the available user tasks (for example, writing a message, sending a message, retrieving mail, printing a message, updating an address list, and exiting the E-mail system) are displayed on the bottom of the screen. To move from one task to another, the user simply uses the mouse to click on the appropriate icon.

While visibility is particularly important for new users, it can become cumbersome after people learn a system. The E-mail icons that showed new users precisely what to do may be nothing more than screen clutter after a few months. Therefore, a system should also be designed with *shortcuts* that let more experienced users move quickly from one part of the system to another. For example, users of an on-line service can "point-and-click" a series of icons to retrieve a weather report, or they can type go weather to jump directly to that part of the system.

Exhibit 4.3 provides a sample checklist that can be used to evaluate a system's navigation interface. After you rank each item, you will know whether this aspect of the system is likely to cause learning problems for users. Remember that when a system has a cumbersome navigation interface, users become cantankerous at the time and effort required to get from one part of the system to another. The irony is that they often don't know where they're going—unless they know where they're going. Any problem areas you find should be targeted during your training.

Assessing the Explanation Interface

All systems have a presentation, conversation, and navigation interface. Not all systems have an explanation interface—although all should. The explanation interface is a system's way of reaching out a helpful hand to users. Protection and forgiveness are two key characteristics of well-designed explanation interfaces. A system with adequate *protection* guards users against making serious errors. For example, if a user attempts to exit from an

EXHIBIT 4.3. Usability Assessment Checklist:
Navigation Interface.

#	What to Look for	Always	Sometimes	Never	N/A
1	The method for moving around within a single screen or dialogue box is simple, obvious, and consistent.	☐	☐	☐	☐
2	The method for moving from one screen to another (or one system function to another) is simple, obvious, and consistent.	☐	☐	☐	☐
3	In GUI (graphical user interface) systems, the method for switching between windows is simple, obvious, and consistent.	☐	☐	☐	☐
4	In GUI systems that use a mouse or other pointing device, users can either click on objects directly or use keyboard shortcuts.	☐	☐	☐	☐
5	Menus are broad (there are many items on a menu) rather than deep (there are many menu levels with a few items on each).	☐	☐	☐	☐
6	The system uses icons, menus, or other navigational aids in a consistent way to help new users move around the system without getting lost.	☐	☐	☐	☐
7	Experienced users can bypass these navigational aids and use shortcuts to quickly jump from one part of the system to another.	☐	☐	☐	☐

application while the unsaved spreadsheet "Year-end Budget" is open, the system might display the message Save changes to Year-end Budget before quitting? (Y,N). In some work settings, the system might be set up to prevent users from deleting critical data.

While protection is especially important for new users, *forgiveness* is essential for experienced users. It is the nature of human beings to make mistakes—and the best systems recognize this and compensate for it. For example, a user working on a complex illustration accidentally presses an incorrect key and half the drawing rotates forty-five degrees. Such an error could cost this user hours of work to correct—but fortunately, she can simply select the undo command and the drawing flips back to its original orientation.

On-line help is an important part of the explanation interface. While more and more systems these days come with some form of on-line help, the content and design of this help is often disappointing. For example, when the user is in the product code field and presses the <HELP> key, the resulting message should say more than This is the product code field! The user knows what field he is in. He wants the system to display a list of available product codes. Also, too many on-line help functions simply answer the question, "What is this?" rather than "How do I. . . ." Users want what they want, when they want it. On-line help needs to provide what they want—or users won't use it at all.

Exhibit 4.4 provides a sample checklist that can be used to evaluate a system's explanation interface. After you rank each item, you will know whether this aspect of the system is likely to cause learning problems for users. If a system's explanation interface (especially its on-line help feature) is strong, you may be able to reduce the amount of required training. But don't make the mistake of assuming that simply because a system has on-line help you can eliminate training completely! At the very least, users need to be taught how to access on-line help and how to use it to answer their questions.

EXHIBIT 4.4. Usability Assessment Checklist: Explanation Interface.

#	What to Look for	Always	Sometimes	Never	N/A
1	The system prevents users from making serious, unrecoverable errors.	☐	☐	☐	☐
2	The system warns users if they are about to take an action that may have serious system consequences.	☐	☐	☐	☐
3	Users can easily and consistently reverse their actions by using an "undo" function.	☐	☐	☐	☐
4	When a user makes an error, the system explains the cause of the problem and the action the user must take to correct it.	☐	☐	☐	☐
5	The system provides an accessible and easy-to-use on-line help system.	☐	☐	☐	☐
6	The content of the on-line help system is accurate, informative, and complete.	☐	☐	☐	☐
7	The user interface (presentation, conversation, and navigation) of the on-line help system is consistent with the user interface of the rest of the system.	☐	☐	☐	☐

Back to the Trenches

Remember Paul? He's the trainer who was given responsibility for PictoTrack training. Everyone told him that the system is easy to use and that only minimal training will be necessary. Paul realized that he'd better get a walk-through of PictoTrack as soon as possible and find out for himself. Here's what he discovered when he assessed the usability of the system.

PictoTrack Strengths

PictoTrack does indeed have some strengths. Its presentation interface is everything Felicia and her graphic artist say it is. There is plenty of white space on each screen, color is used effectively, icons are distinctive, and window management is a breeze. The conversation interface is also pretty good. Care was taken to use the same terminology as the old warehousing system, so personnel won't need to learn a new language. System messages are generally clear and informative, and the system provides feedback most of the time.

PictoTrack Weaknesses

PictoTrack's major weaknesses are in its navigation and explanation interfaces. These are the problems that Paul found:

1. The system has thirty-eight different data entry screens, and each one can be reached only via a series of hierarchical menus. Because these menus are deep (having many levels of menus, with a few items on each) rather than broad (having a few menu levels with many items on each), users must work their way down through at least six menus to get to a data entry screen.

2. There are no shortcuts to permit experienced users to jump directly to a screen, and Paul keeps getting lost in the levels of menus. He keeps wishing that he could play Hansel and

Gretel, leaving a little trail of bread crumbs to lead him back from the depths of the system. He imagines the users will feel the same frustration.

3. While the system provides adequate feedback, it offers virtually no protection. Paul thought he'd faint when he accidentally pressed the <DELETE> key instead of the <DUPLICATE> key and an entire book order vanished. Fortunately, he was only working on the test database, but warehouse personnel wouldn't be so lucky.

4. The much-touted on-line help system is, to put it kindly, underwhelming. Although it is accessible at all times (there is a dedicated <HELP> key on the keyboard), it doesn't provide much useful information. For example, when Paul moved the cursor to a field labeled "date" and pressed <HELP>, the explanation on the screen read: This is the date field. When Paul couldn't figure out how to print a partial order and did a keyword search on the term print, all he found was a two-sentence description of the print command.

5. The user interface of the on-line help system is not the same as the user interface elsewhere in PictoTrack. In the rest of Picto-Track, users press the <ENTER> key to leave a screen. The on-line help system uses the <TAB> key for the same purpose. Paul suspects that this will confuse users. Also, while in the rest of PictoTrack the color red indicates an error condition, the on-line help system uses red letters to indicate words that can be looked up in a glossary. Paul is pretty sure that users will panic when they press the <HELP> key and see all that red.

Using the Assessment Results to Target PictoTrack Training

How will this information help Paul as he plans the PictoTrack training? First, since Rodney and Tomàs have made it clear that Paul has a limited amount of classroom time at his disposal, he can be sure that he devotes that time to the navigation and explanation interfaces. He doesn't need to waste time showing students the individual data entry screens, since each is well-designed. Instead, he can concentrate on teaching students the cumbersome steps required to get to these screens. Second, he can make sure that he warns students about the serious consequences of pressing the <DELETE> key. Finally, since his usability assessment uncovered huge gaps in the online help system, he may be able to convince Rodney and Tomàs to let him develop a more comprehensive user guide.

What's Next

So far, the chapters in Section Two have looked at ways to select the content of your training. Chapter Three focused on the people who will use a system. This chapter has described a method for finding the strengths and weaknesses of the user interface, to help you target your training to the parts of the system that may cause problems for learners. Finally, what you teach will depend on how the system will be used on the job. Chapter Five takes a step back and examines the work environment in which people will use the system.

Environment

5

Assessing the Work Environment

Know Your Setting

Report from the Trenches: Baggit, BizWhiz, and Boris

Baggit is a Portland-based company that makes backpacks, canvas totes, and soft-sided luggage. They have fifty full-time employees and an additional thirty-five contracted stitchers who are paid by the finished piece. The company has been in business for five years. While the manufacturing end of the business has always run smoothly, financial management used to be a mess. For the first three years, Baggit relied on expensive accounting and database software from two competing vendors, as well as an outside service for billing. It used cash register receipts to track sales. Then, two years ago, Baggit purchased a site license for BizWhiz, a multiuser program that combines sales, marketing, inventory, and finance functions. This off-the-shelf application is aimed at small businesses, and includes additional groupware features such as meeting scheduling, appointment tracking, and messaging. BizWhiz also produces financial statements, charts, and graphs, which provide the company with up-to-date information on company transactions and records.

BizWhiz has made a world of difference. Now that all Baggit software is essentially "under one roof," the company's financial management process flows smoothly. However, Baggit has traded one difficulty for another. Every new hire needs to learn how to use BizWhiz. Since the company is so small, it does not have a training department; and since BizWhiz has so many functions, it is extremely time-consuming to learn. The solution? Boris! Boris is Baggit's top salesman and a closet techno-dweeb. He has been with the company for three years. Before that, he spent five years as a systems analyst for a major software developer, until the pressure of impossible deadlines caused him to develop peptic ulcers. Boris greeted Baggit's purchase of BizWhiz with delight, and put in many overtime hours learning all its features and quirks. As a result, he knows more about BizWhiz than anyone else in the company.

So, Boris has become the unofficial BizWhiz trainer. Whenever a new employee is hired, he or she spends a day with Boris for an intensive overview of the software. Unfortunately, one day isn't nearly long enough to do justice to the depth and breadth of BizWhiz; but one day is all that's available, because Baggit needs Boris out on the road generating sales. Boris does his best: he starts at the main menu and explains one function after another until he runs out of time or his trainee runs out of patience. Is there a better option? Hold that thought—we'll return to Boris at the end of the chapter. To help him solve his problem, we need first to address how to examine the environment in which people use a system to do their jobs.

Why Assess the Work Environment?

We have seen that computer training begins with content: since you can't teach it all, you have to teach what's important. We have also seen that determining course content depends on several variables. So far, this section of the book has examined two of these variables: the learner and the system. This chapter examines the third piece of the puzzle: the environment in which learners will use the system.

Let's say you are teaching a course on PressPower, a sophisticated page layout program. You have analyzed your learners, following the recommendations in Chapter Three, and have determined that they are both system savvy (they have used other software applications but are new to PressPower) and task savvy (they have a graphics background and some skills in manual pasteup). You have also used the checklists in Chapter Four to assess PressPower's usability, and you know which parts of its presentation, conversation, navigation, and explanation interfaces are complex and likely to confuse learners.

Your next set of questions should focus on the work environment: How will your learners use PressPower to do their jobs? Do they create newsletters? Brochures? Books? Scientific publications? The course is going to look different depending on the way the software will be used. For instance, if the work environment requires the production of newsletters, people will need to know how PressPower handles multiple columns, links text blocks across pages, vertically aligns text across columns, and wraps text around graphics. Conversely, if the work environment expects people to produce books, they will need to know how to use PressPower to create an index and table of contents, number pages automatically, and manage multiple chapter files. In either of these work environments, learners will probably need to set up style sheets.

Three Dimensions of the Work Environment

As noted earlier, whenever technology is introduced into an organization, there is a ripple effect across all jobs and work processes in that organization.[1] Some systems are universally advantageous: they let everyone get more done in less time and with less effort. Other systems make life easier for some parts of the organization while demanding extra energy from others. And some systems seem to require everyone to work harder. This chapter will help you to assess the work environment along three dimensions: frequency of system use, task complexity and criticality, and degree of end-user support (see Figure 5.1). By examining each of these dimensions, you can ensure that you will teach your learners what they will actually need to do their jobs.

FIGURE 5.1. Dimensions of the Work Environment.

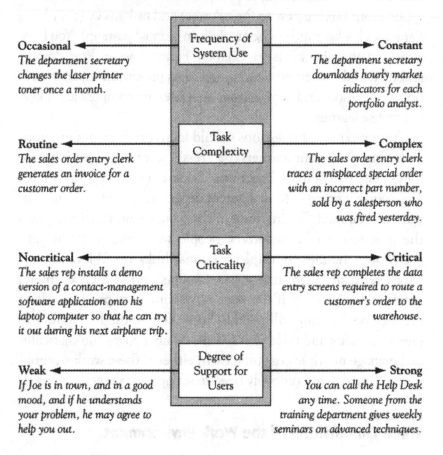

Occasional ◄──────── **Frequency of System Use** ────────► Constant
The department secretary changes the laser printer toner once a month.   *The department secretary downloads hourly market indicators for each portfolio analyst.*

Routine ◄──────── **Task Complexity** ────────► Complex
The sales order entry clerk generates an invoice for a customer order.   *The sales order entry clerk traces a misplaced special order with an incorrect part number, sold by a salesperson who was fired yesterday.*

Noncritical ◄──────── **Task Criticality** ────────► Critical
The sales rep installs a demo version of a contact-management software application onto his laptop computer so that he can try it out during his next airplane trip.   *The sales rep completes the data entry screens required to route a customer's order to the warehouse.*

Weak ◄──────── **Degree of Support for Users** ────────► Strong
If Joe is in town, and in a good mood, and if he understands your problem, he may agree to help you out.   *You can call the Help Desk any time. Someone from the training department gives weekly seminars on advanced techniques.*

How Often Will Learners Use the System?

The first thing you need to find out about the work environment is the frequency of system use. In other words, how often must people use the system to accomplish their jobs?

Constant Use. In some work environments, learners use the system *constantly* once training is complete. Constant use means that people interact with the system for several hours a day, and that this interaction is an integral part of their jobs. Examples of constant use include the following:

- Data entry clerks use the insurance company's claims processing system eight hours a day to set up, maintain, and track customer claims.

- Stockbrokers use the brokerage firm's portfolio management system from the time the London market opens until the Tokyo market closes.

- Hospital admissions personnel use the patient billing system to register two hundred patients a day.

Frequent Use. In other work environments, while learners will not use the system constantly, they will use it *frequently*. Frequent tasks are performed regularly and often, and learners typically use many system functions every week. Examples of frequent use include the following:

- Attorneys use the firm's E-mail system once or twice a day to send interoffice memos.

- University faculty use a word processor five to ten hours a week to write memos, lecture notes, and scholarly articles.

- Sales staff spend two hours every week using contact management software to maintain their client lists, and an hour a day using the same software to prepare for sales calls.

Occasional Use. Finally, some work environments will require only *occasional* system use. In these environments, learners use the system now and then, and may only use a few system functions each time. It may instead be that the system as a whole is used frequently but certain functions are only used once in a while. Examples of occasional use include the following:

- A department secretary uses the office scheduling system for an hour each day, but she prints an appointment calendar only once a month.

- A graduate student uses the college library's research database only once or twice an academic quarter, the day before a paper is due.

- The graduate student's mother uses a personal financial program every week to write checks and keep track of her family's expenses, but she only archives the year's expenses at the end of December.

Applying This Information to Your Training. Once you have identified constant, frequent, and occasional system tasks, how do you apply that information to your training? Ensuring that constant and frequent tasks are done efficiently has an enormous productivity payback. If you can show a stockbroker how to retrieve portfolio data quickly and easily, you will be helping her get more information to more clients in a more timely fashion. If you can show a salesperson how to update his client lists more quickly, he will have more time to spend selling his products. Because mastering constant and frequent tasks has such a large personal and organizational benefit, it makes sense that these tasks should be the focus of your training. Also, training on these constant and frequent tasks can often be accomplished quickly because the new skills are immediately and continually reinforced on the job. So, for example, it may take three days to teach new hospital admissions staff how to operate the patient billing system. However, once they get back to the admitting office, they will use the system eight hours a day, and will be adept by the end of the week.

Occasional tasks are not as good a bet for formal training, since learners are likely to forget the skill before they have a chance to use it. For instance, if you teach the department secretary to use the office scheduling system on October 2 but she doesn't have to print the appointment calendar until October 31, you can be quite certain that she will call you in a panic on October 30. Occasional tasks are better addressed by user guides or on-line help systems, which can provide the required information just when the user needs it. Remember, however, that such support materials are only useful if they can be easily accessed. Chapter Seven will discuss how to design clear, accurate, and relevant support materials.

How Complex and Critical Is the Job?

Another important dimension of the work environment is the complexity and criticality of the job. Every job consists of many different tasks.[2] For example, a technical trainer's job might include such tasks as developing exercises, writing end-of-course test questions, photocopying course materials, delivering instruction, and evaluating student performance. A legal secretary's job might include such tasks as taking messages from clients, typing legal briefs, resolving scheduling conflicts, and sending out bills. As these examples show, if you want to understand the complexity of a job, you need to have a sense of the tasks that constitute that job. In other words, when people use a system to carry out their jobs, do these jobs consist of tasks that are routine, complex, or a combination of the two? Also, how critical are these tasks?

Routine Tasks. Routine tasks are easily broken down into steps that are done the same way and in the same order every time the task is performed. Examples of routine tasks include the following:

- Backing up the computer's hard drive to floppy disks
- Alphabetizing the firm's client list and generating a set of mailing labels
- Setting up bank accounts for a new customer

Complex Tasks. Complex tasks are the opposite of routine tasks. When a task is routine, the information needs that it generates will be very similar each time the task is undertaken. When the task is complex, the exact information needs cannot be known in advance and will vary unpredictably from one occasion to another.[3] Because they are done differently every time, complex tasks defy breakdown into discrete steps. A complex task may be performed only once in the lifetime of a job—for example, developing a budget for the relocation of the company's headquarters from San Francisco to Pacific Grove—or it may be performed often, with the individual steps, decisions, and end results changing each time it is performed—for example, developing marketing plans for new-product launches. Examples of complex tasks include the following:

- Figuring out why the computer's hard drive crashes every time the backup program is run

- Designing a customized database that will be used to track the firm's clients

- Correcting a system glitch that occasionally causes bank customers to be charged 88 percent interest on their auto loans instead of 8.8 percent

Critical Tasks. Finally, whether a job consists of complex tasks, routine tasks, or a combination of the two, it is important to determine which of these tasks are critical. Critical tasks support essential business goals, such as when the vice president of finance uses a financial modeling tool to assess first quarter earnings, preparatory to approving next year's budgets. Critical tasks must be performed properly; failure to do so may result in equipment failure, data loss, financial costs, or even personal injury. *Noncritical tasks* have less impact on the success of a business. For example, it is probably not a critical task when the same vice president of finance fiddles around with type styles and colors in the budget report. Errors in the performance of noncritical tasks, while bothersome, are not devastating. Consequently, it is important for training to emphasize the critical tasks, whether these tasks are complex (for example, designing a marketing brochure to launch the company's newest product) or routine (for example, generating monthly billing statements).

Applying This Information to Your Training. Once you understand the complexity and criticality of all the jobs in the work environment, you can design training and support materials that take this information into account. Table 5.1 provides examples of training appropriate for various types of tasks. For example, if you are teaching people whose jobs consist largely of complex tasks, you may want to consider a problem-based training approach. Give learners a scenario that they are likely to encounter back on the job, and have them use the system to work through the scenario. A sales rep might be told the following: "Your customer wants to know what it would cost and how long it would take to special order a thousand units of our product in royal blue. Log on to the main system and find out the answer." A medical student might be given the following scenario: "You are managing a case of measles in a seven-year-old boy who has AIDS. Use the *Index Medicus* database to find five journal articles that discuss possible treatment complications due to drug interactions."

If you are training people whose jobs consist largely of routine tasks, make sure that your instruction provides opportunities for hands-on practice. If a routine task consists of a great many steps and you are concerned that your learners may forget crucial steps or perform them in the wrong sequence, you may also want to give

TABLE 5.1. Assessing Tasks to Decide How to Teach.

	Task Is Critical	Task Is Not Critical
Complex Task	Training with an emphasis on case studies to enhance problem-solving skills	On-the-job coaching when the user is ready to perform the task
Routine Task	Training that gives learners a chance to perform the task and to practice using job aids	Little or no training; instead, the details should be documented in a user guide

learners a job aid or a detailed user guide. Such written support materials are generally easy to develop, since the sequence of steps in a routine task does not change. Have learners practice the task exactly the way it will be done on the job, using the support materials to guide their practice. This is especially helpful if learners can take these support materials back to their desks after training.

How Much End-User Support Is Available?

A final aspect of the work environment that will influence your training is the degree to which users are supported after training. In some organizations, end-user support is weak: people who are sent off to learn a computer system are basically on their own once they return to their jobs. In other settings, end-user support is strong. In these work environments, training is only the beginning of the learning process: people and/or materials are in place to help users solve problems and improve skills.

Support May Come from People.   People are one type of end-user support. These people may include informal coaches and help-desk personnel. A coach is typically a co-worker who provides system advice and troubleshooting as needed. Coaches become coaches because they know the system better than anyone else in the office, so new users gravitate toward them when they encounter problems. Some organizations even formalize the coaching process. For example, after classroom training is finished, each new bank teller may be assigned to work under the supervision of an experienced teller for a month.

In organizations with help desks, users can call a central phone number when they have system questions. This approach is similar to coaching in that users get the information they need when they need it. However, since help-desk personnel are usually system experts, this type of end-user support can be more comprehensive than coaching. Some organizations routinely track the types of questions received by the help desk; trainers can then use this information to determine the content of their training. For example, if the help desk receives thirty calls a week from users who can't figure out how to format mailing labels, it is probably worthwhile for the trainer to include this task in the course; or if the task is already being taught, the trainer should probably come up with a better way of teaching it.

Support May Come from Materials. Materials are the other type of end-user support. These may include written documents (such as user guides and job aids) as well as on-line performance support (such as detailed system messages and context-sensitive help). Although most systems these days provide some form of written support material, the quality of these materials can vary radically from business to business and from system to system. Assuming for a moment that these written materials are accurate and accessible, it is essential that learners get an opportunity to use them while they are learning the system. The same is true for job aids, which are generally one- or two-page "cheat sheets" of important system commands and procedures. Unfortunately, in many cases learners don't receive these support materials until the last day of training! If you want people to look up information in a user guide or a job aid, you need to teach them to do so while you are teaching them to use the system. For example, if you are doing one-on-one instruction and your student asks you a question, you might respond by saying, "That command is described in the job aid; why don't you try to find it there first." If you are teaching a group, you might design an exercise that asks learners to find the section of the user guide that explains how to create a new spreadsheet formula and then to follow these written procedures to set up their own formula.

On-line performance support systems are becoming increasingly common. However, just as with written support materials, some on-line materials are better than others. In other words, moving information from the three-ring binder to the computer screen does not automatically guarantee quality: if the content is useless or out-of-date, it won't magically become more beneficial if it's put on-line!

However, if a system's on-line help is accurate, informative, and easy to use, it can be a good vehicle for continual learning, allowing users to improve their skills after training is over. The recommendation for user guides and job aids also applies to on-line performance support: if you want learners to refer to on-line support *after* training, you need to give them a chance to use it *during* training. For example, a training exercise might have learners first look up the term "margins" in the on-line help glossary, then jump to the on-line procedure for changing margins, and then follow the procedure to change the margins in their own documents.

Back to the Trenches

If Boris wants to maximize his day of one-on-one training with new Baggit employees, his best bet is to take a look at the tasks these employees must accomplish on BizWhiz. Here is what he would learn:

1. Only the Baggit office manager uses the meeting management function—and she uses it only once a month. All sales people use the order entry and customer tracking function for at least two hours a day. The vice president of finance runs financial tracking reports once a week. The bookkeeper and other financial personnel post billing information daily. The warehouse staff check inventory several times a day.

2. The majority of BizWhiz tasks are routine. For example, posting a sales order consists of five steps that never vary. The weekly sales report is generated automatically. The only complex task is the procedure for tracking lost shipments—and Boris always handles this procedure himself. While most tasks are routine, nearly all are critical to the success of the business. For example, if orders are not posted correctly, then inventory figures are incorrect and the company winds up with either shortages or overstock.

3. End-user support consists of Boris, an on-line help system, and a user guide. Boris is great, of course, but he spends most of his time on the road. Fortunately, the on-line help system is both accessible and comprehensive. Users can look up all BizWhiz terms, commands, and procedures in plain English, and can easily switch between their work and the help system. The user guide is also well-designed, although it weighs several pounds. Every system function is documented in enormous detail, and there is both a table of contents and an index to help users go directly to the page they need.

With this understanding of the work environment, Boris should be able to focus his single day of training on the parts of the system his learners will be using most often. Since no one can possibly learn BizWhiz in one day, he should also consider spending at least an hour teaching new employees how to use the on-line help system and user guide. With a carefully selected overview of the system and an understanding of how to use the support materials, new employees will be able to master BizWhiz independently, even after Boris goes back on the road.

What's Next

This chapter concludes Section Two of the book, in which you learned how to determine the content of your training by performing a needs assessment of the learners (Chapter Three), the system (Chapter Four), and the work environment (this chapter). Section Three turns your attention from *content* (what to teach) to *process* (how to teach it). Chapter Six discusses how people learn: it shows you how to make your training efficient, effective, and memorable. Chapter Seven describes how to use instructional materials to support and supplement your training.

SECTION THREE

How Should I Teach It?

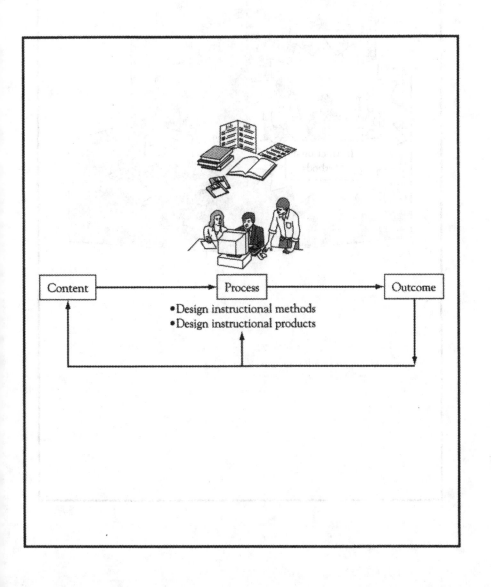

Instructional
Methods

6

Selecting
Instructional Methods

Telling Isn't Teaching

Report from the Trenches:
The Bumpy Road from Tech Writer to Trainer

Gurus to Go (G2G) is a computer training firm that specializes in running public seminars on business software applications. Yolanda is their newest instructor. Before taking the job with G2G, Yolanda was a technical writer and documentation designer for a small software development firm. She eventually tired of producing user guides that nobody read, and she thought training would provide a nice change of pace. Although she had never taught before, the G2G personnel manager decided to hire her because of her expertise on Design-O-Page, the popular page-layout program.

Last week, Yolanda flew to Kansas City to teach her first Design-O-Page public seminar. Since she knows the software so well, she spent very little time preparing; she figured she could basically "wing it" once she got there. Now that the class is over, she is astonished at how hard she had to work and how exhausted she feels. While the class was not precisely a disaster, she thinks it could have gone much better. For one thing, she did most of the talking. She kept encouraging her students to ask questions, but they rarely raised their hands. Although some of the participants spent the entire day looking confused, they never asked for her help. Also, the time seemed to get away from her. For instance, she had planned to spend only fifteen minutes explaining how to set up master pages, but she got so involved in the material that an hour flew by before she realized what was happening. Finally, she senses that participant energy was low all day, though she can't quite articulate how or why it happened. Despite all this, when Yolanda handed out the standard G2G evaluation form at the end of the day, her instructor rating was 4.1 out of a possible 5. She knows this will please her supervisor, but she has a sinking feeling that the rating is higher than she deserves. None of the participants complained, but no one was particularly enthusiastic either. She wonders how many of these participants will actually use Design-O-Page when they get back to their offices.

Yolanda is scheduled to teach three Design-O-Page seminars a month for the next five months. Because of her Kansas City experience, she realizes that there is more to teaching than standing in the front of the room and talking. She is determined to improve her skills so that her upcoming classes will be more satisfying—to her and to her students.

What Happens When People Learn to Use Computers?

If you want people to learn a lot and to like what they have learned, you need to understand how the brain works when it acquires new information. Entire library shelves are devoted to different (and often conflicting) theories of human cognition, and it is beyond the scope of this book to do justice to the topic. The purpose of this part of the chapter is merely to give you a brief overview of what happens in the minds of learners when they learn to use computers. When you build a house, you need to start with a sturdy foundation. When you teach people to use computers, you also need to start with a foundation—one that guides your decisions about how to design and deliver training. This overview will serve as that foundation.

People Learn by Interacting with the System

It is important to start by recognizing that users do not respond passively to a computer system. They are continually interacting with it by framing goals (what they want to accomplish), intentions (how they want to accomplish it), and expectations (what the outcome will be). They make mistakes and try to draw conclusions about how the system works from the way it responds to those mistakes.[1] Each interaction leads to a more clear, complete, and accurate mental model of how the system works. The more interactions the user experiences, the better the user's mental model will be. In other words, accumulating a body of knowledge about how the system worked in the past lets users make predictions about how the system will respond in the future.[2] Computer-use training, therefore, needs to give learners a chance to have many interactions with the system.

People Learn by Transferring Knowledge of Other Systems

Computer-use training also needs to acknowledge and build on learners' experiences. When people learn to use a system, they are in a continual process of refining their understanding. By making their knowledge efficient, they move from the stumbling state of the naive user to the smooth, practiced skill of the experienced user.[3] Learners expedite this process by applying what they already know about other systems. For example, learners who already understand the concept of templates from their experiences with a word processor can apply the concept to a page-layout program, which also uses templates. Learners who can format text in a word processor will have an easier time figuring out how to format text in a graphics application, even if the two programs perform this function in entirely different ways. The more familiar learners are with computer systems, the more efficiently they will learn a new system. This process is known as *transfer of knowledge*. So, when it is said that users "understand" how a system works, it means they are able to solve problems that are different from what was explicitly taught.[4] In other words, they can transfer their knowledge to new situations.

People Learn by Establishing Relationships Between Internal and External Tasks

In addition, computer-use training must help learners to understand the relationship between what they want to accomplish (*external task*) and how they must interact with the system to accomplish it (*internal task*).[5] When people are first learning to use a system, this relationship is often confusing. How many times have you heard a frustrated user say something like, "I know what I want to do, but I don't know how to explain it to the &¢ %@$ computer! I wish it would just let me talk to it in plain English." This person has not yet learned how to connect his external task to the system's internal task. He might describe the external task like this: "A customer called me up and said she needed to change her order from twelve pairs of navy socks to fifteen pairs of green socks. I have to get the change to the warehouse quickly, before they send out the afternoon shipment." While this is the way an order entry clerk would frame the task in his own mind, he will need to frame it differently to get the job done on the system. The internal task might go something like this: (1) Select `Existing Order` from the main menu. (2) Type the customer's last name and order number. (3) Press the `<SEND>` key. (4) When the `Order` screen appears, press the `<TAB>` key until you are in the field that needs to be changed. (5) Type in the new information (and so on).

People Learn by Using Systems to Solve Problems

Finally, computer-use training often needs to help people use systems as problem-solving tools. As computer systems have increased in sophistication and capability, they have moved well beyond their function as data storage and retrieval devices. In the past, most learners simply needed to learn a system's data entry rules; these

TABLE 6.1. A Problem-Centered Orientation to Computer Training.

Phase	Description	Example
Planning	Recognize and define a problem, identify processes to solve the problem, and organize these processes into a unified strategy.	"We've just introduced five new products and want to get the word out as soon as possible. Do I add sales staff, increase print advertising, or go for an all-out media blitz? How do I use the system to select the best strategy?"
Problem representation	Decide how to articulate the information critical to the problem.	"The system will let me design a customized report to find out how a 20 percent increase in sales staff this quarter will impact my department's profitability for the year, assuming a 30 percent increase in sales due to introduction of the five new products."
Self-monitoring	Evaluate the results of implementing the solution, and refine as needed.	"According to the report I just ran, I can't justify adding staff. Let's try another scenario. What happens if we maintain current staffing levels and increase print advertising?"

days, they need to know how to use a system to solve complex problems. Since adults' readiness to learn is affected by their need to
know or do something, they tend to have a life-, task-, or problem-
centered orientation to learning rather than a subject-matter
orientation. They don't want an explanation of each system command; they want to know how to create a budget, print an enve-
lope, or design a brochure. Table 6.1 shows that a problem-centered
orientation to computer training includes planning, problem rep-
resentation, and self-monitoring.[6]

Three Things to Keep in Mind About Adult Learners

If you want people to learn a lot and to like what they have learned,
you need to recognize the ways adults and children differ, and
account for the "adultness" of your learners.[7] Adults are people with
histories, attitudes, and a lot to lose if they fail. When you teach
people to use computers, it is important to harness three characteristics of adult learners: their rich body of life experience, their agendas, and their tendency to be self-directing.

Adults Have a Rich Body of Life Experience

Children are aware that they haven't been around for very long. As
a result, they put a rather low value on their experiences. Adults,
however, take pride in the fact that they weren't "born yesterday,"
and are eager to test new concepts and skills against what they
already know. Many learners are system savvy: they have used other
systems in the past. Others are task savvy: they have done their jobs
for some time, even if these jobs have not included the use of computers. Computer-use training needs to build on these experiences,
since people learn best when they see the relationship between
what they already know and what they are attempting to learn.

Remember Yolanda's Design-O-Page seminar described at the
beginning of this chapter? If she opens her workshop with participant introductions, she can quickly determine the proficiency of

the learners. She can then make use of this information throughout the day, drawing parallels between their experiences and the skills they need in order to use Design-O-Page. For example, suppose she discovers that none of the participants has ever done page layout. While this may not sound too promising, it is certainly true that everyone in the class has read a newspaper, received a brochure, and filled out a form; if Yolanda is creative, she can find ways to describe all of the concepts and skills required to master Design-O-Page in terms of these three kinds of documents.

Adults Have Agendas

The movie "Peggy Sue Got Married" shows an adult Peggy Sue transported back in time to her high school algebra class. When her teacher reprimands her for daydreaming during his explanation of quadratic equations, she snaps back "I don't have to learn this! I know *for an absolute fact* that once I graduate I will never use it." Children may be satisfied when teachers tell them that information will be useful in the vague future, but adults are not nearly as compliant. They have come to training because they want to accomplish something, and if they don't get a chance to accomplish it, then no matter how articulate and engaging you are, they will not be satisfied.

The best way to plan for learner agendas is to conduct a needs assessment well in advance of the training. Section Two of this book describes needs assessments in detail. By discovering what learners want to get out of training, you can be sure to address skills that they will find meaningful. In Yolanda's case, however, this is not possible. Public seminars are difficult settings in which to meet all participants' agendas, because the instructor has no control over who attends and no interaction with these participants in advance of the seminar. Yolanda has to hope that the G2G brochure has accurately described the goals and objectives of her Design-O-Page workshop, and that participants have selected this workshop because the content meets their needs.

Adults Tend to Be Self-Directing

Cast your mind back to your first day of kindergarten. You used crayons when it was coloring time, played on the swings when the class went out to the playground, drank your milk at snack time, and took a nap when the teacher said you had to. What did you know? You were only five, and this was the way the world worked. Big people told little people what to do and little people obeyed. Adults are different. They learn best when they can control the pace of their learning, so exercises should be provided that let learners work independently. They also want to use what they learn shortly after they learn it, so what you teach should conform to what they will do as soon as training is over.

During her Design-O-Page workshop, Yolanda might want to use some alternative exercises to let participants work on the skills that best match their job descriptions. Some learners may plan to use Design-O-Page to set up technical articles, others may intend to use the program to design one-page ads, while still others may be responsible for book design. To meet the diverse needs of her participants, Yolanda could prepare three different exercises. One exercise might provide practice in setting up information in tables, a second might emphasize the placement of graphics, while a third might focus on manipulating large blocks of text. Participants could then select the exercise that teaches the skill they need most.

Theory Is Nice—But What Do I Do on Monday?

So far, this chapter has examined what happens when adults learn to use computers. The idea was to give you a theoretical foundation upon which to construct your training. Now let's get practical. You have five senior-level managers meeting you in the conference room on Monday morning. They want an overview of the company's E-mail system. Their goal is to leave the conference room with the ability to send, receive, and print messages without asking their secretaries for help. Since they are busy folks, they only have two hours to spare.

Well, OK. You know the E-mail system better than anyone else in the company. But how do you explain it so that these managers will understand it and feel secure enough to actually use it? As shown in Table 6.2, whenever you teach people to use computers, you should work toward three goals: meeting individual differences, fostering active learning, and building learner independence. The rest of this chapter will describe how to create training that achieves these goals.

TABLE 6.2. Goals of Computer-Use Training.

Design training to:	Using these strategies:
Meet individual differences	• accommodate different learning styles • accommodate multiple skill levels
Foster active learning	• provide the appropriate level of challenge • control the teaching-learning process • use questions effectively • encourage students to track relevant information
Build learner independence	• encourage active exploration • increase students' locus of control • design relevant and challenging exercises

Designing Training to Meet Individual Differences

It has been said that there are two types of people: those who classify people into two types, and . . . well, you get the point. It is certainly true, though, that trainers encounter far more than two types of learners. A class of five students is not a single entity; it is five individual human beings, each with a unique combination of learning style and skill level. Failure to account for these differences virtually ensures that some of your learners will get left in the dust, while others will yawn themselves into a stupor. By recognizing the individual differences among your learners, you can make sure you have planned strategies to accommodate them.

Accommodating Different Learning Styles. People learn in different ways. Some learners, when confronted with a new software application, just start fiddling with it until they understand how it works. Others don't even turn on the computer until they have spent several hours reading the user guide. Some learn best when they are given the freedom to work on their own projects, while others feel more secure using a predefined set of steps to solve an instructor-designed exercise. Some people benefit greatly from team projects; others get cranky when forced to work in teams, preferring to practice on their own. Some can tolerate a high level of chaos and uncertainty, while others need a great deal of structure and instructor guidance.

Whether you teach primarily individuals or groups, it is important to recognize these individual learner differences and to make sure that your training accommodates them. A good way to start is by becoming aware of your own learning style. Do you learn best in a team or on your own? Do you tend to learn a new system one step at a time, or do you prefer to plunge right in and try to solve a work-related problem? There is no right or wrong learning style, but problems can occur if you make the mistake of assuming that everyone else learns the way you do.

Suppose you are teaching those senior-level managers how to create an E-mail message. Since you learn best by tackling problems head-on, you might explain the basic procedure and then say, "OK, now give it a try and holler if you get stuck." For the managers whose learning style is like yours, this teaching strategy is appropriate. In fact, a more structured approach would make them feel stifled. But the strategy will not work for the managers who learn best by following written instructions. They will probably feel abandoned and demand more of your attention—at which point you may start to feel like a baby-sitter. Because of these learning style differences, you really ought to be prepared for both types of learners. You might still begin by asking everyone to work independently on a project, but you should have in mind a plan for how you will help those learners who prefer more structure. Some managers may feel uncomfortable asking for help directly, especially in front of their peers, so pay attention to nonverbal cues. Be alert to any managers who exhibit signs of unease or frustration, and offer to work with them. You may begin by helping one manager in this way, and find that after a few minutes you have two or three others clustered around you. This flexible approach lets all your students master new skills in the way they learn best.

Accommodating Multiple Skill Levels. A major headache for computer trainers is teaching groups that include both naive and experienced users. In an ideal world, beginning and advanced students would not attend the same training session; in the real world, they often do. Dealing with multiple skill levels is a problem with no perfect solution. Some trainers pair up students—an experienced user with a naive one. They justify this strategy on the grounds that the naive user will get individualized help and the experienced user won't be bored. In the spirit of the adage that "to teach is to learn twice,"[8] the experienced user may even benefit from being a helper. (Think of the last time you taught someone to use a system. In the process of familiarizing yourself with the information, organizing your thoughts, preparing exercises, and fielding learner questions, chances are you learned considerably more than your students, who were simply passive recipients.) While this is often true, pairing an experienced and naive user has two major disadvantages. First, the quality of the training can be jeopardized, since computer expertise does not guarantee teaching expertise—which is, as you may recall, the raison d'être of this book! It is also unfair to the experienced user, who presumably is attending training not to teach but to improve his or her skills.

Another strategy some trainers use to handle multiple skill levels is the one practiced in elementary schools from time immemorial. Remember reading groups? There were generally three: the bluebirds, the pigeons, and the vultures. The teacher met with each group individually, pacing her instruction to the ability level of the students. Some trainers mimic this strategy: they do a quick assessment of participant skills and then divide the class into beginner, intermediate, and advanced groups. They lecture to the beginners, provide structured exercises for the intermediates, and allow the advanced students to work on their own projects. This approach occasionally is appropriate in week-long workshops, in which participants have plenty of time for independent practice. It is considerably less effective during short training sessions, because none of the three groups will receive enough of your time. A more serious problem with putting students into groups is the tendency of trainers to leave a student in the "vulture" reading group forever. While some students will start the session with few skills, they may catch on quickly and be ready for more advanced exercises as the training progresses.

I do not recommend either pairing naive users with experienced users or splitting your class into bluebirds, pigeons, and vultures. Instead, I recommend handling multiple skill levels by establishing your objectives and expectations at the start of the training session. State clearly what skills you plan to teach, so that all participants will know what to expect as the training progresses. Openly acknowledge that your participants may not be at the same skill level, and state your intention to assist all levels to the best of your ability. Explain what strategies you will use to accomplish this goal, so that neither the experienced nor the naive users feel ignored. This acknowledgment assures learners that, while their proficiencies may differ, they will all be treated with equal respect.

Once you have articulated your training strategy, get through the basics at a brisk pace. While naive users may flounder a bit, you will lose the attention of experienced users if you spend too long on rudimentary information. Instead, plan to give naive users extra attention throughout the training to help them catch up. One way to monitor individual needs is to create a "parking lot" on a flip chart, where students can post questions and concerns. Make it a point to address these concerns sometime during the session; by the end of the day, all questions should be out of the parking lot. Finally, provide multilevel exercises and allow participants to complete these exercises at their own pace.

Designing Training to Promote Active Learning

When teaching people to use computers, it is desirable to give them ownership of the learning process. Some learning theories go so far as to state that until the learner has this ownership, little useful learning will occur.[9] Ownership is achieved when people are active participants in the teaching-learning process rather than passive recipients of information. What can you do to foster active learning?

Providing the Appropriate Level of Challenge. The first strategy is to create a learning environment that provides the appropriate level of challenge without causing undue stress. Acquiring the knowledge and skills required to master a new computer system is always somewhat threatening, especially for adult learners. Since too much stress can interfere with learning, your goal should be to create a safe haven for your students. Put students at ease right from the start by acknowledging that a certain amount of stress is natural. Throughout the training, continually reinforce the message that questions are welcome and confusion is okay. Conversely, too little stress is as bad as too much. While too much stress can cause anxiety and interfere with learning, too little stress can cause boredom: learners will simply tune you out. The ideal learning environment creates a balance that is "just right": enough stress to challenge learners and stimulate their interest without causing panic attacks. Think of this as the Goldilocks Paradigm.

Controlling the Teaching-Learning Process. The second strategy to encourage active learning is to make sure that you are in control of the teaching-learning process. While this strategy may initially seem like a deterrent to active learning, control is not the same as rigidity. Learners need structure and ground rules. Learners need to know what you expect of them and what they can expect of you. This principle may sound familiar: it is the touchstone of a healthy family. Maintaining control of your training means developing a schedule and, within reason, sticking to it. Many computer trainers make the mistake of thinking that, because they know the system better than anyone else, they can simply "wing it." The result is that they spend most of their time either lecturing or responding to student questions, and are left wondering where the time went. Your goal should be to routinize your teaching. In other words, you should be so familiar with both the material and the sequence of your instruction that you can use most of your energy to encourage student participation and address individual concerns as they arise.

Using Questions Effectively. The third strategy is the use of questions to actively engage learners. Questioning is an essential training technique because it establishes two-way communication between a teacher and learners. The creative use of questions also encourages communication among students, thus reinforcing group interaction and cooperative learning. The following guidelines are adapted from *Instructor Excellence: Mastering the Delivery of Training.*[10]

- *Provide correct and concise answers to participant questions.* In other words, when a participant asks a question, be accurate and brief in your response. Don't elaborate unnecessarily. If you don't know the answer, don't make one up; students will see through this in no time and your credibility will suffer. You are always better off saying something like, "Actually, I've never used this program to typeset mathematical formulas, but I'll check it out during our next break and get back to you before lunch."

- *Refer participant questions back to the group when appropriate.*
  This is a good way to promote group interaction. For example,
  if Jill asks, "How do I get these columns to line up correctly?"
  and if you think others in the class could benefit from solving
  this problem, you might reply, "Has anyone else run into that
  situation? How did you handle it?" Realize, however, that this
  approach needs to be used with care. If you turn every participant question back to the group, students may decide that you
  aren't doing your job.

- *Use open questions to solicit responses from participants.* Such
  questions as "Why do you think you got that error message?"
  or "Now that you know how to set up tables, how many
  different ways might you use them?" open up discussion
  among learners.

- *Give participants enough time to respond to your questions.*
  It sometimes takes a minute for learners to translate your
  question into terms they understand, then to frame their
  response, raise their hands, and get ready to speak. Learn to
  pose a question and tolerate silence until your participants
  are ready to respond.

- *Use closed questions to end discussions.* Important as discussions
  are, if you want to maintain control of the training, you can't
  let them go on forever. Closed questions, such as "Are there
  any more questions about setting up tables before we move on
  to our next topic?" are appropriate to use at the end of a discussion or exercise. Questions framed in this way give participants one last chance to clarify a point or resolve an issue
  before moving forward.

Encouraging Students to Track Relevant Information. Finally,
consider a "techniques and applications" log (see Exhibit 6.1) to
help students keep track of information that they particularly want
to remember back on the job. You may have overheard your students saying things like "That split-column trick you just showed us

would be a great way to do the masthead for the monthly newsletter" or "You mean the 'Outline' command can be used to move rows up and down in a table? Cool. Now, if only I can remember it when I get back to work." Encourage students to jot down these little discoveries in their individual logs. This technique is especially useful for learners who have been away from formal schooling for some years, and who may be out of the habit of extrapolating from general principles to personal applications. The simple act of maintaining a personal document sharpens students' attentiveness to what is going on in the training session. It encourages active learning by encouraging trainees to look for useful ideas throughout training rather than waiting until they are back on the job and then relying on their memory.[11]

EXHIBIT 6.1. Techniques and Applications Log.

Technique (What I Learned)	Application (How I Plan to Use It)
Use the SORT command to alphabetize a list of names in a table (put last name first)	The student registration lists for the course instructors
Switch to OUTLINE view to move rows up and down in table	Revising the job sheets
Paste a spreadsheet into the document with the OBJECT command (automatically updated whenever you change spreadsheet information)	The monthly budget report This will be a big help!

Designing Training to Build Learner Independence

Whether you are teaching one student or a group, whether your training lasts two hours or two weeks, the reality is that any learning that occurs on your watch is just the beginning. The bulk of the learning process will take place after training is over, as students begin to use the system back on the job. Consequently, a critical goal of training is to get participants ready to learn on their own. Rather than simply teaching *about* computers, you should be teaching your students *how to learn about* computers.

Encouraging Active Exploration and Experimentation. One way to achieve this goal is to encourage active exploration and experimentation. Give participants opportunities to make mistakes in a punishment-free environment, so they will learn that nothing terrible happens when they mess up. This assumes, of course, that nothing terrible *does* happen! In other words, experimentation only works with systems that provide protection and forgiveness. For example, if you are teaching a colleague how to use a well-designed spreadsheet program, you might have her select a column and press the <DELETE> key. Whoops! The column vanishes. Before she becomes hysterical, you show her how to use the Undo command to get her work back. Chances are that once she sees she can recover from mistakes she will have the courage to try out other system features when she is working on her own.

Increasing Students' Locus of Control. A second way of increasing learner independence is to use teaching methods that gradually shift the locus of control to your students. Locus of control is a concept that simply answers the question "Who's in charge here?" Think of a squad of new recruits in Army basic training: the locus of control rests firmly with their drill sergeant. When teaching a new skill, use the following four-step approach to increase your students' locus of control:

1. *Begin with a demonstration.* For example, you might demonstrate how to set up a master page with two columns, a header, and a footer. When you use this method, the locus of control is in your domain. You are in charge of the teaching-learning process, since you are presenting the information and your students are simply receiving it.

2. *Give your students a chance to practice the skill.* For example, design an exercise that has students create a master page with two columns, a header, and a footer. The locus of control has shifted somewhat toward your students, since they are actively engaged. However, they are not yet independent, since they are merely mimicking the steps you demonstrated.

3. *Provide the opportunity for performance "on a leash."* For example, design an exercise that has students creating a publication whose left and right master pages are different. The locus of control is now moving even further toward the students, since they must now apply the skill you demonstrated to a new situation. They are "on a leash" because you are available to give individualized feedback.

4. *Provide the opportunity for performance "with a parachute."* For example, let each student design his or her own publication. The publication can be of any length but must use master pages and multiple columns. Explain that while you will be available if they become hopelessly muddled, you won't answer questions that can be found in the user guide. Now the locus of control is entirely with the students, since they are in charge of deciding how to apply the skill. They are performing "with a parachute" because you are available if they encounter serious trouble.

Designing Relevant and Challenging Exercises. A third way to increase learner independence is through the use of carefully crafted exercises. Such exercises must be both relevant and optimally challenging. *Relevant* exercises let students practice the skills that they will have to perform when training is finished. For example, if you are training a group of high-level executives to use the company's meeting management system, it is probably not useful to include an exercise on how to print monthly departmental calendars if this task is handled by the department secretaries. A more relevant exercise for these learners would be for them to practice using the system to schedule their own meetings.

Optimally challenging exercises maintain a delicate balance between too much stress and too little. To reduce the amount of stress, make sure you have already taught students the basic skills they will need to complete the exercise. For example, if an exercise is designed to teach the skill of moving a paragraph from one part of a document to another, students should already know how to open a document and scroll through long text blocks. To increase the amount of stress in an exercise, have students practice performing a skill that is slightly different from the one you demonstrated. For example, if your demonstration shows how to place a graphic in the middle of a page, the exercise might require students to wrap text around a graphic in a three-column publication.

What's Next

This chapter has addressed the issue of how people learn. It has described methods to make your training efficient, effective, and engaging, so that students will learn a lot and like what they have learned. These methods, while helpful, are not sufficient. When people learn to use computers, they do most of the actual learning not in the classroom but back on the job. Since you can't follow your students to their desks and watch over their shoulders while they do their work, you need to provide materials that they can refer to when they want to improve their skills. Chapter Seven describes the use of instructional materials to supplement your training and support your learners.

7

Selecting Instructional Products

Support Materials That Really Support

Report from the Trenches: Well-Schooled

Fumiko runs the computer room at the Yardsley Middle School. During school hours, little groups of students in grades five through eight rotate through the room, using computer-based training programs to practice basic math and reading skills. Under pressure from the Yardsley school board to justify the school's investment in all this technology, the school principal has decided that faculty need to be using these computers as well. Last week he called Fumiko into his office. First, he complimented her on the breadth and depth of her computer expertise, while she waited patiently for him to get to the real purpose of the meeting. Eventually he got around to asking her to help the Yardsley teachers use the computer room equipment to create overhead transparencies and instructional handouts. "Two or three in-service sessions ought to bring them up to speed," he concluded.

Fumiko has taught elementary school students for three years but has never led an in-service session. Given the limited amount of training time available, she knows she can't teach her colleagues everything—so she starts with a needs assessment to figure out what is most important. This is what she has discovered about the learners, the system, and the work environment:

- *The learners.* All fifteen Yardsley teachers are task savvy. They are experienced practitioners who have created hundreds of overhead transparencies and instructional handouts. Eleven of the fifteen are system aware, having only minimal experience with computer systems. The remaining four are system savvy; they have used word processing software, and one is experimenting with on-line services.

- *The system.* The software in the computer room is a bit of a mixed bag. Some of the programs are old and not as easy to use as their newer counterparts (which the school has not found the funds to purchase). Other programs are state-of-the-art, but they take time and effort to master. The best of the bunch is the presentation package: it is easy to learn, fun to use, and lets users create stunning overhead transparencies in minutes.

- *The work environment.* Yardsley teachers will use the equipment in the computer room once a week, at most. Since students occupy the room throughout the school day, the teachers will have access only before 8:00 A.M. and after 3:00 P.M. The tasks for which teachers will use the computers are complex, since every handout or transparency is a new design problem to be solved. However, these tasks are not critical: the school can function quite nicely without computer-generated instructional materials. The support for the teachers consists solely of Fumiko—when and if she is available.

The assessment of the learners and the system has given Fumiko useful information to guide her training. The assessment of the work environment has left her scratching her head. While she is delighted to help her colleagues, it is clear that in this setting a few in-service sessions will not transform them into skilled computer users. For one thing, since the teachers will only use the machines in the computer room occasionally, they are likely to forget from one visit to the next everything she has taught them. Since they will be using these machines to do complex work, it is impossible to predict which parts of the software they will use on any given day. To make matters worse, while Fumiko will provide as much end-user support as possible, she isn't willing to put in long hours after the school day is over. Teachers who want to use the computer room after 4:30 will just have to manage on their own. The assessment of the work environment has led her to an important conclusion: she will have to provide support materials to supplement her in-service sessions.

Three Types of Support Materials

When you teach people to use computers, it is important to recognize that many of their skills will be developed after formal training is over. This chapter examines three types of support materials that can enhance and supplement training: user guides, on-line help, and job aids. The first two generally come with a system and can vary widely in their quality and effectiveness. This chapter will help you decide whether the user guides and on-line help that accompany a system can be a helpful adjunct to your training. While you are stuck with the user guides and on-line help you are given (unless developing these materials is part of your job), job aids are something you can design yourself. This chapter will explain when and how to create job aids to help learners remember infrequent, complex, or critical procedures. Finally, the chapter will show you ways to incorporate all three types of support materials into your training.

User Guides

Everyone who has ever used a computer is familiar with user guides. These are typically book-sized documents that describe all system commands, functions, and procedures. User guides are ubiquitous. They come with all off-the-shelf applications, and generally accompany software that is developed internally for use within a company. If truth be told, no user ever sits down and reads a user guide from cover to cover. (Actually, people who write user guides for a living sometimes wonder if anyone ever reads a user guide at all!) Instead, user guides support users by serving as reference materials, to be opened only when a user runs into trouble.

To be truly serviceable, user guides should be organized by job or task rather than by system function; that is, they should describe what the user might want to accomplish with the system. They should also be small enough to fit easily on a user's desk. Complex programs may have several user guides: a reference manual that contains all commands, a procedural manual that gives step-by-step instructions for each user task, and a troubleshooting manual that explains how to recover from error conditions. Whether a system comes with one user guide or many, you have probably observed that some user guides are better than others. They vary widely in their accuracy, completeness, and usability. But unless your organization considers it your job to rewrite these materials, you (and your learners!) will simply have to cope with what you get.

On-Line Help

On-line help is another type of support material that you generally have to accept as is. When it is well-designed, on-line help is an efficient way to get information to users just when they need it, without requiring them to thumb through a user guide. Because software companies are maneuvering for market share, most commercial software these days has on-line help features. On-line help is even becoming prevalent in systems that are developed internally. Unfortunately, just as with printed user guides, there is enormous variation in the quality of on-line help. This is a pity because once users interact with one poorly designed or inadequate help facility, they are unlikely to try another. Even if you are teaching people to use a system that has decent on-line help, you may need to overcome some learner resistance before your students agree to use it.

Several types of on-line help are possible. They differ in the way the user asks for information and in how much information they contain. They can range from simple systems with a single help display to complex help facilities that lead users through large on-line manuals. Examples of on-line help include the following:[1]

- *Error messages.* These are displayed when the user makes a mistake (Unable to complete print request). They may also provide diagnostic information about why the error may have occurred, and procedural information about what the user can do to fix it.

- *Context-sensitive help.* The information displayed depends on where a user is in the system when help is requested. For example, requesting help in a data entry field displays a list of available product codes. Requesting help while executing a command displays an explanation of the command.

- *On-line reference manual.* Some help facilities link context-sensitive help to an on-line version of the complete reference manual. For example, when a medical student asks for help while performing a keyword search, the help facility displays the relevant portion of the *Index Medicus* reference manual. The student can then read further in the reference manual to learn how to do other kinds of searches.

- *Active or diagnostic help.* These "smart" help facilities intervene if the system detects that the user is confused. For example, some word processing programs are designed to automatically correct typographical errors. More-sophisticated systems "watch" the user and attempt to provide guidance. For example, a financial management program detects that the user has typed the name of a security that has not previously been defined. Rather than displaying an error message, the system responds: Security JANUS 50 does not exist. Do you want to create it? and displays a dialog box to set up the new security.

Job Aids

Writing user guides and developing on-line help are probably not within your purview (and are certainly beyond the scope of this book). Developing job aids, however, is a skill that can serve all computer trainers in good stead. Giving your learners well-designed job aids to bring back to their desks after training may make the difference between training that works and training that doesn't. Job aids—also known as performance aids, quick-start guides, tip sheets, or cheat sheets—are brief documents that remind users of key commands and procedures. (They can also be displayed on the screen rather than on paper, at which point they become on-line help.) Whereas user guides are designed to be comprehensive, job aids are deliberately concise. Exhibit 7.1 shows an example of a job aid.

Job aids are not new. In the years before 1984, long-distance operators (at what was then the only telephone company in the country) had voluminous three-ring binders crammed with all company policies and procedures. These documents typically sat on shelves gathering dust, since they were too bulky to move and too confusing to read. So, how did the operators do their jobs? They made themselves little notes about important procedures and slipped these notes under the sheet of glass that covered their desks. These personal crib sheets, known as "the underglass," were job aids. They were especially effective because they had been designed by the people who knew their jobs best: the operators themselves.

Whether tucked under glass or taped over a computer keyboard, job aids can benefit computer users in several ways:[2]

- *Job aids give users permission to forget.* For example, a vice president who runs quarterly budget reports only four times a year

EXHIBIT 7.1. Sample Job Aid: Hints for DOS Commands.

Hint	Example
* is a wildcard.	copy a:*.* b:
File names are eight characters or less.	myreport
File names can be followed by a three-character extension.	myreport.txt
Leave one space between commands.	save myfile a:

will probably not remember the sequence of steps to follow. Giving this vice president a job aid that jogs her memory suggests that she is not expected to remember how to perform this occasional task. It also frees her to concentrate on learning the parts of the system she uses more often.

- *Job aids help users manage vast quantities of information.* For example, an inventory management system may require data entry clerks to use a hundred or more complex codes, each representing a different product. Posting a list of these codes in plain sight reduces the need for memorizing. It also decreases the likelihood of data entry errors.

- *Job aids close the gap between training and task performance.* For example, a medical librarian may have only an hour to show ten medical students (who are already challenged by an overwhelming curriculum) how to use the *Index Medicus* to search the medical literature. The librarian has time to demonstrate key features of the system, but the students won't have a chance to practice doing searches under his supervision. However, if he develops a job aid of the important search commands, and spends part of the session teaching the students to use this job aid, they will be able to carry out medical literature searches on their own.

- *Job aids designed by users reinforce key teaching points.* The most powerful job aids are the ones users design themselves. For example, the radiological technician in the nuclear medicine department uses highly sophisticated software to analyze bone scans. Since she uses the equipment every day, she rarely refers to the extensive manuals that sit on a shelf in her office down the hall. However, now and then a patient needs a special type of scan that is handled differently by the software. To ensure that she doesn't make any errors during this critical and complex procedure, she has copied the relevant page from the user manual and highlighted the essential steps in yellow (to make them readable in the low lighting conditions of the treatment room). She has laminated the page and taped it to the side of the computer monitor.

Characteristics of Effective Support Materials: Content and Design

When you teach people to use computers, it is important to assess the quality of the available support materials. All support materials—user guides, on-line help, and job aids—need to be examined in terms of their *content* and their *design* (see Exhibit 7.2), to determine whether these characteristics make them beneficial to learners. If you discover that a system's user guides and on-line help are well-designed, you can use them to supplement your training. If they are not well-designed, you will know that you can't rely on them to help to help learners improve their skills, and that job aids may be necessary. Even if you determine that user guides and on-line help are adequate, you may still design job aids to target the job-specific needs of your learners. In either case, the criteria for effective content and design can help you develop useful job aids.

Examine Support Materials for Content

Some years ago, a presidential candidate drew on the refrain from a fast-food hamburger commercial to challenge his opponent with the question, "Where's the beef?" The issue was style versus substance: he claimed that his opponent was doing a lot of talking but not saying much. Computer support materials must have "beef" as well. Four-color graphics and eye-catching layout are useless if the content isn't in place.

Computer users need user guides, on-line help facilities, and job aids that are accurate, complete, relevant, and clear. It is most important that they be *accurate*, because if users encounter errors in a job aid or user guide, they are unlikely to use the document again. Support materials must be *complete* for the same reason. There is nothing more frustrating than searching a three-hundred-page user

EXHIBIT 7.2. Criteria for Effective Content and Design
of Support Materials.

Area	What to Look for		Always	Sometimes	Never
Content	Accurate:	Information in the product is free of errors.	☐	☐	☐
	Complete:	The product contains everything a user may need to know about the system.	☐	☐	☐
	Relevant:	Information is pertinent to the tasks people will perform on the system.	☐	☐	☐
	Clear:	The product is written in a way that is understandable to readers.	☐	☐	☐
Design	Easy to navigate:	The product contains navigational aids such as an index, page numbers, or hypertext links.	☐	☐	☐
	Quick to scan:	The product uses layout techniques such as white space, typographic cues, and consistent formatting.	☐	☐	☐

guide for information and coming up empty-handed. Completeness is especially important for user guides and on-line help; job aids are deliberately incomplete, since they only contain critical or easily-forgotten information. The information in support materials must also be *relevant*. For example, the user guide for the company's payroll database should not contain procedures for database backup if the only user who will ever back up the database is the system administrator. Finally, user guides, on-line help, and job aids must always be written in a way that is *clear* to readers.[3] Technical terms should be avoided wherever possible. Essential technical terms should be defined. Sentences should be short and to the point. Procedures should be broken down into steps, and each step should be described in a way that makes sense to nontechnical users.

Examine Support Materials for Design

While content is critical, it is not sufficient. If the content is not accessible, support materials are nothing more than an information dump. I have a friend who works at the receiving end of a software company's technical support hotline. He spends his days fielding calls from confused, frustrated, and occasionally nasty people who can't get their software to behave. Easily half the time my friend has to bite his tongue to keep from advising these callers to "RTM." RTM isn't a technical term: it's shorthand for "read the manual," which these callers don't do. Ironically, the answers to their questions are often *right there in the user manual*—somewhere. Why don't people turn to user guides and other support materials when they get stuck? Often it is because these materials are poorly designed.

Computer users need user guides, on-line help facilities, and job aids that can be easily navigated and quickly scanned. They must be *easy to navigate* so that users can find their way around them with little difficulty. This is generally not difficult to accomplish with job aids because they are concise documents. User guides, which are much heftier, need mechanisms to get users to the right page in a timely manner. They may include a table of contents and an index, although studies on documentation use show that users refer to these only about 25 percent of the time. More often than not, users simply flip through pages to hunt for information.[4] This result suggests that designers should use page numbers, headings, and other visual cues to assist users. These cues should be part of on-line reference manuals as well. Embedded cross references are another mechanism that supports navigation in lengthy documents. For example, the page that explains how to format text might also refer users to the page that describes how to format graphics. In an on-line document, this referral can be accomplished with a hypertext link: clicking on the cross-referenced procedure will bring users to the explanation of that procedure. It is essential for on-line help to have the same navigation methods as the rest of the system it supports. For example, if in the rest of the system users press the <ENTER> key to move from one screen to another, the system's on-line help facility should not use the <ESCAPE> key for this purpose. Users must also be able to switch easily between the help facility and their work, and should be able to resume their work where they left off.

After using navigation techniques to get to the right section of a user guide, on-line help document, or job aid, users must be able to *quickly scan* to find the information they need. With scannable support materials, readers know how to process information simply by the way that information is formatted on the page (or the screen). An ideal format is one that requires the least amount of processing by readers.[5] There are a number of layout techniques that support scanning. One of these is the systematic use of white space to make each "chunk" of information stand out. Text headings also help users read selectively. For example, the next section of this book is called "When to Design Your Own Job Aids." In the future, when you are ready to design a job aid, you can scan Chapter Seven and use the heading to find this information quickly. Finally, typographical cues such as bold text, large type, and arrows can draw the reader's attention to important information. While these cues can assist scanning, the more cues are used, the less helpful they are.

Think of the junk mail that overflows your mailbox in November and December, each ad shouting louder than the next for your attention. After a while you begin to tune them all out. To maximize the effectiveness of typographical cues, ten percent or less of printed or on-line text should be formatted in this way.[6] In addition, each cue should represent only one thing throughout the document.[7] For example, if a red arrow alerts users to potentially dangerous error conditions, it should not also highlight terms that are defined in the glossary.

When to Design Your Own Job Aids

This chapter has been examining three kinds of support materials: user guides, on-line help, and job aids. Of the three types of materials, job aids are probably the type that you will actually develop yourself. User guides and on-line help generally come with the software. Although job aids sometimes come with software, too, they are often more useful if you customize your own. And since all you need in order to design a job aid is a piece of paper and a decent word processor, it makes sense for you to develop job aids that are targeted to your audience.

This is not to say that job aids are mandatory; they are only appropriate under certain circumstances. When can job aids be helpful tools to support computer users? You should consider designing a job aid if the following conditions, which have been adapted from *A Handbook of Job Aids*,[8] exist:

- System functions are used occasionally, are critical, are complex, or have multiple steps that must be taken in an invariable sequence.

- The consequences of errors are high.

- The performance of a system task depends on a large body of information, or on information that changes frequently.

- There is high turnover among system users.

Job aids can also compensate for design flaws in a system's user interface. Consider the following scenario: A catalogue company's order entry system requires data entry clerks to type incomprehensible product codes each time a customer calls to place an order. Because each product has a different code, the clerks are continually making data entry errors. This slows down the order-taking process, frustrates the clerks, and exasperates the callers. Training can't solve the problem, because turnover among the data entry clerks is high. Ideally, of course, the system should never have been built this way. It should have been designed to either eliminate these codes entirely or display a list of the appropriate codes when the clerk presses a dedicated <HELP> key. However, a job aid like the one in Exhibit 7.3, while not a perfect solution, can help remind data entry clerks which codes to use for which products.

Take another look at the job aid in Exhibit 7.3. Does it meet the content and design criteria described earlier in this chapter? Sure. Will it help the data entry clerks enter the correct product codes? I have no idea. Job aids need to be tested to see if they work. The only way to assure yourself that a job aid truly supports users is

EXHIBIT 7.3. Sample Job Aid: Product Codes.

To order this type of product...	Use one of these product codes	
Kitchen Utensils	PFTB540L	Large tongs
	PFTB540S	Small tongs
	PFTB777	Carving knife set
	PFTB854r	Vegetable peeler (red)
	PFTB854b	Vegetable peeler (blue)
Pots and Pans	EN1247	12-inch covered skillet
	EN327	Omelet pan
	EN520	Nonstick wok
Cleaning Supplies	PGC767B	Brass polish
	PGC767S	Silver polish
	PGC982C	Carpet stain remover

to find some users, put them in front of the system with the job aid beside them, and then sit back and watch what happens. You may think you have developed a job aid that is a model of clarity—and you may be right. But if users fumble around looking for the command they need, or are unable to follow the sequence of steps as you wrote them, then you will need to make revisions.

It is important to test a job aid with a representative sample of users. That is, you need to find a group of users whose proficiency level closely matches that of the people who will eventually use the job aid. Let's say you have developed a job aid that summarizes the commands for the company's E-mail system. If the people who use the E-mail system are primarily experienced users, your job aid should be tested on experienced users. While naive users would probably find the job aid confusing, their opinion isn't relevant since they are not your target. However, if E-mail users fall everywhere along the continuum from naive to experienced, your job aid must be suitable for all these proficiency levels. In that case, you need to be sure you have tested the job aid with the appropriate mix of users.

Back to the Trenches: Getting People to Use Support Materials

This chapter has discussed how appropriate user guides, on-line help facilities, and job aids can supplement your teaching. It has also described how these same materials can support your users after training is complete. While there are exceptions, most support materials contain valuable information that can help users when they run into trouble. However, when users have questions, they generally proceed in this order: try and see what happens; ask another user; call the vendor; search the on-line documentation; read the manual.[9]

So, why do most people resist using support materials? Technical writers and instructional designers have been struggling with this dilemma for years. Countless theories have been proposed, contradicted, and abandoned. There is no simple answer. But doesn't it at least make sense that if you want support materials to be used, you have to teach people how to use them? I maintain that *teaching people how to use a system should always include teaching them how to use the support materials that accompany the system.*

At the beginning of the chapter I introduced Fumiko, who realized that she had better supplement her in-service training with support materials. Here are the strategies she adopted to encourage Yardsley teachers to use each of the three types:

1. Low OverHead, the presentation software, comes with a comprehensive *user guide*. Although the information in the guide is complete, it is not always easy to navigate. During the in-service session that deals with making overhead transparencies, Fumiko uses an exercise that requires the teachers to add color to a transparency. She hasn't taught this skill directly, but the steps are described quite well in the user guide. When she reviews the exercise with the teachers, Fumiko explains that they must refer to the user guide in order to complete the exercise. She emphasizes that despite its accessibility problems the user guide is a good source of information, and even makes a little joke, saying "You can't judge a book by its cover, or even its index, but trust me—the information is all in there." A few teachers grumble a bit at having to do their own reading, but by the end of the session most agree that the procedures in the user guide are clearly written and easy to follow.

2. Picasso, the graphics software, is a powerful program with a long learning curve. Yardsley teachers will probably use only ten percent of the program's features, and even this is too much to cover during a two-hour in-service session. However, the program does have comprehensive *on-line help* that lets users learn as they go. Therefore, rather than explain how to use the program, Fumiko decides to spend the session teaching her colleagues how to use the on-line help. Before class, she creates a file containing a humorous drawing of a frazzled-looking teacher with a huge stack of papers on her desk. She introduces the session by having her students display the on-line help facility as they click on each part of the drawing.

She then shows them how to switch between the drawing and the on-line help, so they can see that their work doesn't disappear. She demonstrates a trick for making the drawing window a little smaller so that the on-line help window is visible at all times. Finally, she gives them a chance to use the massive on-line reference manual. She has them do a keyword search on the term "scale" to see how the program makes objects larger or smaller. She also explains how to use hypertext links to jump from the "scale" command to other related procedures. By the end of the session, Fumiko is confident that any teacher who really wants to will be able to use the Picasso on-line help.

3.   Writer Rooter, the word processing software, is an outdated program with some very odd design "quirks" and an incomprehensible user guide. To compensate for these flaws in the software and the manual, Fumiko designs a one-page *job aid* summarizing the commands that Yardsley teachers will use most often. During the in-service session that deals with designing handouts, Fumiko posts an enlargement of the job aid at the front of the room. She also makes a copy of the job aid for each teacher. Every time she refers to one of the commands on the job aid, she points to its location on the enlargement. Whenever the teachers work on an exercise, she reinforces their use of the job aid by saying things like, "To make text double-spaced you need to use the 'DS' command, which is explained on the job aid." After a while this gets to be a running gag with the teachers, who start chanting "which is explained on the job aid!" right along with her. Still, by the end of the day Fumiko thinks she has gotten the message across. And if she's lucky, the teachers will refer to the job aid when they have questions rather than come running to her.

What's Next

This chapter concludes Section Three of this book, which has addressed strategies you can use if you want people to learn a lot and to like what they have learned. These strategies include instructional methods (Chapter Six) and instructional products (this chapter). In Section Four, you will turn your attention from process (how to teach) to outcome (how to tell if it worked). Chapter Eight discusses *evaluating teaching*; it shows you how to use student evaluations and peer reviews to improve the design and delivery of your training. Chapter Nine discusses *evaluating learning*; it shows you techniques for measuring student achievement.

SECTION FOUR

How Can I Tell If It Worked?

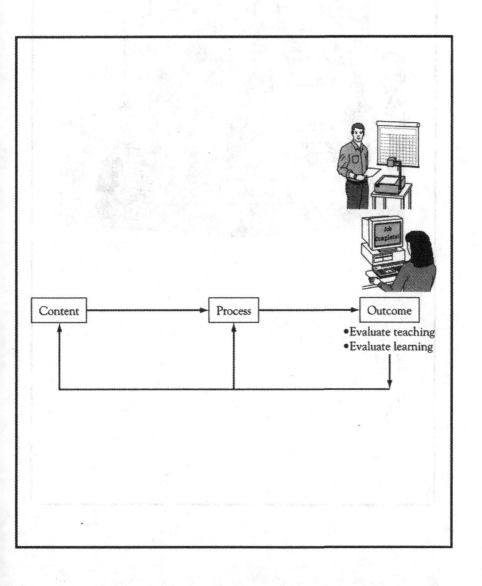

8

Evaluating Teaching

Beyond Smile Sheets

Report from the Trenches: Drummond Beughel Corp.

Drummond Beughel Corp. is the world's oldest management and technology consulting firm. With 4,200 partners and staff in more than thirty cities worldwide, timely information exchange has become a paramount need. To that end, the technology division of Drummond Beughel was given a mandate to develop a company-wide global communications system. They created Know It All, a knowledge base designed to promote collaboration among the firm's key decision makers.

Know It All is an impressive product. It includes E-mail, conferencing, real-time chats, and a comprehensive database with sophisticated search capabilities. "Know It All stimulates the exchange of ideas," said Eva Norman, a principal at Drummond Beughel and one of the architects of the system, in a *Wall Street Week* interview. "It provides our staff all over the world with easy and immediate access to the current information about our business and the experts behind the ideas."

Now that Know It All is available, the 4,200 partners and staff need to learn how to use it. Willem Rosemassen, director of technical training for Drummond Beughel, has been charged with the task. A great deal is riding on this training. Willem has to be sure that the worldwide staff of twenty-three trainers does the best possible job of teaching Know It All. In other words, he has to evaluate. Drummond Beughel has traditionally monitored the quality of their courses with what the trainers call "smile sheets." Distributed at the end of every class, these evaluation forms ask participants to rank, on a seven-point scale, the instructor, the course objectives, the course materials, and the training facility. The same form is used to evaluate all courses, from sales training to project management to advanced C++ programming. The items are then tabulated, summarized, and carefully filed in each trainer's personnel file.

Willem has long believed that while Drummond Beughel is known throughout the industry for its commitment to high-quality training, the company's course evaluation policy leaves much to be desired. He decides to use the rollout of Know It All as an opportunity to develop a more comprehensive evaluation approach.

Why Smile Sheets Aren't Enough

Despite the title of this chapter, there is actually nothing wrong with smile sheets. Although the term is often used in a cynical or pejorative way, it is accurate: smile sheets do indeed tell you if students are smiling at the end of training. This is not worthless knowledge. Student evaluations give you one important piece of information that you can learn nowhere else: *how the students experienced the training*. Only the students themselves know the answer to this question. If students do not react favorably, they probably will not be motivated to learn. Positive reaction to a course may not guarantee learning, but negative reaction almost certainly will interfere.[1]

Student evaluations are a powerful method for evaluating teaching; the problem comes when they are the only method used. Since evaluations are administered at the end of the course, they are more like a snapshot than a movie; they capture the one moment in time when students are filling them out. Student evaluations don't indicate how students felt during the training, or how they are likely to feel after they get back to work and start trying to use what you taught them. Student evaluations also don't indicate whether your course meets generally accepted criteria for effective training design and delivery. Poor courses are sometimes rated high by students, while excellent courses are sometimes rated low. Everyone has experienced a course led by a particularly entertaining or charismatic teacher who, despite his or her energy, actually taught very little. By the same token, while negative student evaluations may point to a problem with the course, other factors completely unrelated to the quality of the teaching may cause students to rate a course poorly. Perhaps these students are resistant to technology. Perhaps they are worried that the introduction of a new system means they will have to work harder.

An effective evaluation requires multiple perspectives. Imagine that you are shopping for a new car. Standing in the showroom, you can evaluate the vehicle from one perspective: appearance. While this evaluation is important, it is not sufficient. You need to take the car out for a road test if you want to evaluate its performance. This adds to your store of knowledge, but it still may not be enough information. For other perspectives, you may read reviews in auto magazines, study the manufacturer's specifications, and even talk to a friend who owns the model. Finally, after gathering as much data as possible, you make an informed, intelligent decision. (You buy the red one.)

Whether you teach individuals or groups, if you are serious about improving your teaching effectiveness you have to evaluate from multiple perspectives. Gathering evaluation data about the quality of your teaching is only worthwhile if you are willing to do something with the results. So ask yourself the question: "What do I want to know about my teaching so that I can do more of what worked and fix what didn't?" This chapter describes three evaluation methods that provide the answers to this question: self-assessment, peer review, and student evaluations.

Using Self-Assessment to Evaluate Teaching

Although there are many sophisticated methods for evaluating teaching, don't overlook a source of information that is always available: yourself! You probably already use this method, whether you know it or not. Every trainer does a certain amount of soul searching after a training session. You may remember Yolanda from Chapter Six: she received good student evaluations for her first Design-O-Page workshop, but had an uneasy feeling that she could have done a better job. She was dissatisfied with her teaching, but she couldn't put her finger on just what was wrong. There is a simple yet powerful technique for making this self-assessment more valuable.

Begin by establishing a set of "success criteria" for your teaching. Sit back and fantasize: imagine that this is the best computer-training class that ever was and ever will be. Imagine that when the class is over you get called to Stockholm for the first-ever Nobel Prize for Teaching. What would be going on during such a class? What would students be saying and doing? Take the time to write down your fantasy. It might look something like the one in Exhibit 8.1.

Once you have established your success criteria, simply be alert to your students' behavior during training. Pay attention to the way they interact with you and with each other. Notice what they say and do. Chances are the reality will fall a bit short of your fantasy

EXHIBIT 8.1. Fantasy of the Perfect Computer-Training Class.

> There is a pleasant hum in the room. Students are excited but intent as they help each other solve problems. At 10:30 they ask if they can work through the mid-morning break so they can learn more features of the system.
>
> Naive students are saying, "I was nervous before this class, but this is really great. I never realized computers could be so much fun!" Experienced users are saying, "Cool! And I thought I knew everything about this program!" The one student who arrived with negative attitudes about the system is saying, "Now that I've seen it in action, I can't wait to try it out on that annual budget report I've been procrastinating about doing. It's going to make all those @$ %& forecasts a breeze!"
>
> At the end of the day, several students come up to me and say that they plan to recommend this course to all their co-workers.

(at the very least, it's highly unlikely that students will give up their morning coffee and donuts!). Nevertheless, predefining these criteria for success gives you a goal to shoot for, and a way to see how close you come to your ideal.

Using Peer Review to Evaluate Teaching

Training is a lonely business. Unlike a number of other occupations, you do not do your work among your peers. Whether you teach individuals or groups, once you close the classroom door (literally or figuratively), it's just you and your students. And while you may think you are aware of everything you do when you teach, chances are you miss a lot. This is why people cringe when they see themselves on videotape. ("Good grief. Do I really stroke my beard twenty times a minute? And I had no idea that I begin every third sentence with the phrase 'Moving right along, folks. . . .'")

Peer review is a method that makes use of fellow trainers to give you feedback about the content and process of your teaching. It is not necessary to use peer review every time you teach a course. This method is especially useful when you are just starting out as a computer trainer, when you have developed a new course, or when you are experimenting with a new teaching technique. In each case, something is new (you, the course, or a technique); peer review gives you a chance to check it out with a knowledgeable colleague. This is not unlike letting your mother read your book report before you hand it in to your third-grade teacher.

When you use a peer reviewer, decide whether you want feedback on *content* (what you are teaching) or *process* (how you are teaching it). The type of feedback you want determines the kind of colleague you ask for help. If you are concerned about the content of your training, bring in a subject-matter expert. This person can determine whether you are teaching the correct information about the system. If you are concerned about process, bring in an experienced trainer. This person can see whether you are presenting the information in an effective way.

Whether your reviewer is a subject-matter expert or an experienced trainer, feedback will be more useful if the reviewer knows what you are especially concerned about. Perhaps you are teaching a system that was just installed last week and you are worried that your grasp of the material is shaky. See if you can get one of the programmers who designed the system to observe your course. Explain that you need to find out whether your explanations of how the system works are complete and accurate. Maybe you have gotten feedback that your lectures seem rushed. Since "rushed" is such a general term, you can't really improve until you know precisely which of your teaching behaviors are causing this student perception. Ask an experienced trainer to observe your course and to pay particular attention to the pacing of your lectures. Ask this colleague to notice how often you stop during the lecture to ask questions and how long you pause for students to respond. If you get the feedback that you ask one question every twenty-five minutes and wait only two seconds before answering the question yourself, you have a problem—and something specific to work on the next time!

Despite the value of peer review, it is not always easy to obtain. Some of your colleagues are teaching classes of their own; others are simply unable to give up the time required to observe an entire teaching session from beginning to end. In that case, try to schedule the review during a representative (or problematic) few hours. Also, keep in mind that some peer review can happen outside the classroom. For example, a reviewer who is an expert on the system may be able to evaluate the content of your course materials and job aids well in advance of training. In fact, such an approach is often preferable since it gives you a chance to correct any errors before you inflict them on your students.

Finally, remember that peer review is hard work for the reviewer. Lots of things go on in a training session, and it's hard to keep track of them all. Chances are your colleagues are not experienced evaluators and may feel unsure of their ability to provide helpful feedback. An evaluation checklist like the one in Exhibit 8.2 can make it easier for someone to review your teaching.

EXHIBIT 8.2. Peer Evaluation Checklist.

#	What to Look for	Strongly Agree	Agree	Neutral	Disagree	Strongly Disagree
1	Trainer appears to understand the course material.	☐	☐	☐	☐	☐
2	Trainer uses a variety of teaching methods.	☐	☐	☐	☐	☐
3	Trainer uses work-appropriate examples.	☐	☐	☐	☐	☐
4	Trainer encourages students' questions.	☐	☐	☐	☐	☐
5	Trainer handles off-topic questions appropriately.	☐	☐	☐	☐	☐
6	Trainer models the use of support materials where appropriate.	☐	☐	☐	☐	☐
7	Trainer checks for learner confusion.	☐	☐	☐	☐	☐
8	Trainer allocates appropriate time for practice.	☐	☐	☐	☐	☐
9	Trainer provides timely and understandable feedback to students.	☐	☐	☐	☐	☐
10	Trainer appropriately manages differences in learner proficiency.	☐	☐	☐	☐	☐

Remember, however, that this is just an example; you need to design a checklist that applies to your own teaching situation.

Using Student Evaluations to Evaluate Teaching

Student evaluations are a third source of data that can help you improve the quality of your teaching. They can give you specific information about what students liked about the training, which may motivate you to do more of the same. For example, if students indicate that exercises were "challenging," "engaging," "useful," and "relevant," chances are good that you will continue to use these exercises in future courses. Student evaluations can also tell you what students didn't like. Negative feedback, while harder to swallow, can lead you to find specific ways to make your teaching better. For example, if students indicate that your lectures were "confusing," "technical," "intimidating," and "abstract," you may be tempted to rail against the wimpy ignoramuses whom you are forced to tolerate in your classroom. Hopefully, though, after you put an ice pack on your ego and calm down, you will realize that since you can't choose your learners, you will have to concentrate on changing yourself. You may even concede your tendency to talk over peoples' heads. Then you can start thinking of creative ways to make the material more accessible to your students.

Numerical Questionnaires

A questionnaire is the easiest way to find out how students perceive your teaching. Most student evaluation questionnaires ask students to rate items on a numerical scale such as the one shown in Exhibit 8.3. The advantage of the numerical questionnaire is that it is quite easy to score. For each item, you multiply the number of responses by the corresponding weighting and add the products together. Then you divide by the number of responses to obtain a final score. Let's say that for item 1 in Exhibit 8.3, the evaluations of a class of twelve students are distributed as follows:

EXHIBIT 8.3. Numerical Scale Questionnaire.

#	How did you feel about the course?	Strongly agree	Agree	Neutral	Disagree	Strongly disagree
1	I found the course exercises to be helpful.	5	4	3	2	1
2	The instructor was knowledgeable about the subject matter.	5	4	3	2	1

Item	Number of Students
5 (strongly agree)	4
4 (agree)	3
3 (neutral)	2
2 (disagree)	3
1 (strongly disagree)	0

To calculate the score for item 1, use the following formula:

$$(5 \times 4 = 20) + (4 \times 3 = 12) + (3 \times 2 = 6) + (2 \times 3 = 6) + (1 \times 0 = 0) = 44$$

Since twelve students responded to the item, divide 44 by 12 for a final score of 3.67.

Free-Form Questionnaires

Numerical questionnaires are easy to score, but free-form questionnaires can sometimes provide more useful feedback. In Exhibit 8.3, item 1 was intended to discover how students perceived the exercises. As you can see, seven students felt pretty good about the exercises, two were neutral, and three didn't like them at all. The final score of 3.67 is not overwhelming in any particular direction. On the average, students didn't hate the exercises, but neither were they ecstatic. Since the purpose of student feedback is to improve your teaching, what do you do with a score of 3.67? How do you know what to improve?

Suppose, however, that you design a questionnaire with freeform questions. Item 1 might instead read like this: "This class used exercises to give you practice using the system. How do you feel about the exercises?" When they answer this question, students use words like "relevant," "useful," and "helpful," but they also say things like "couldn't finish," "rushed," and "lack of feedback." Aha! Now you have some useful information. You know that the exercises themselves don't need to be redesigned; you just need to allocate more time for students to complete them. Since free-form questionnaires are more time-consuming to score, you may want to use this method sparingly. But if a course is new or you are trying out a new approach, this type of questionnaire can be a rich source of data.

Be Selective in What You Ask

Whether you use numerical or free-form questionnaires, resist the temptation to evaluate the universe ("As long as the students are rating things, let's ask them what they think of the new carpeting in the training room"). You will be much better off asking students a few carefully crafted questions that you will actually use. If students believe that their responses will be read and pondered, they are more likely to take the evaluation seriously. This is especially important when you use free-form questionnaires; if you want students to write reflective comments, be sure you don't ask for too many of them. Also, only ask questions if you can do something about the answer. For example, consider the question, "To what extent did this class meet your expectations?" This question doesn't evaluate the teaching—it evaluates the precourse marketing brochure! Suppose students respond that, indeed, their expectations were met. What can you do to ensure a similar rating in future classes, other than hope you have students with similar expectations? And if students respond that the class did not meet their expectations, how do you respond to that feedback? Students may have entered training with unrealistic expectations ("I've never used a computer before and I want you to make me an expert in four hours.") Or they may not have had any expectations—they came to training because they were sent by their manager. A better question might be, "To what extent will the skills you learned in this course help you in your work?"

Exhibits 8.4 and 8.5 show sample student evaluations. Exhibit 8.4 uses a standard rating scale; students simply circle the appropriate number. Exhibit 8.5 combines a rating scale with a place for students to write free-form comments. Such questionnaires can give you the feedback you need to find out what worked, so you can do more of it, and what didn't, so you can fix it. Remember, however, that these are just examples; you need to design a questionnaire that applies to your own teaching situation.

Analyzing Student Responses

After you have distributed and collected your student evaluations, you need to analyze the responses. Some organizations turn this into an extremely complex process, but it need not be. Let's say you distribute a questionnaire like the one in Exhibit 8.5, and out of twelve students, four describe the course design as "too formal," three as "overly technical," and three as "rigid." Ten out of twelve is a strong enough trend to take this assessment seriously. However, if only three out of twelve react that way, you probably should not rush to redesign the entire course—at least see what happens the next few times you teach it. Also, when you analyze student responses, it is wise not to overreact to hotly worded comments. Statements like "Instructor is a megalomaniac" or "If this training had been a dress, I'd return it" should be treated as judges treat gymnastics events: throw out the highest and lowest scores. (This is

EXHIBIT 8.4. Know It All Course Evaluation:
Standard Rating Scale.

We need your input to determine the effectiveness of the Know It All training. Please give us your reactions, and use the back of this form to make additional comments or suggestions.

Instructions: Please circle the appropriate response after each statement.

#	How do you feel about the Know It All course?	Strongly Agree	Agree	Neutral	Disagree	Strongly Disagree
1	I learned a lot about how to use Know It All.	5	4	3	2	1
2	Know It All will help me do my job at Drummond Beughel better.	5	4	3	2	1
3	The course was organized in a logical sequence.	5	4	3	2	1
4	The course was conducted at an appropriate pace.	5	4	3	2	1
5	The trainer was knowledgeable about the subject matter.	5	4	3	2	1
6	The trainer presented the material in a professional manner.	5	4	3	2	1
7	I had opportunities to be actively involved in my own learning.	5	4	3	2	1
8	Working with a "training buddy" was a useful way to learn the system.	5	4	3	2	1
9	The user guide and job aids will help me as I use Know It All.	5	4	3	2	1
10	I would recommend this course to other Drummond Beughel partners.	5	4	3	2	1

EXHIBIT 8.5.   Know It All Course Evaluation:
Combined Rating Scale and Free-Form Questions.

		High				Low
Instructions: Please circle the appropriate number after each statement and then add your comments.						
#	Reaction					
1	How do you rate the course content (relevance, interest, etc.)? Comments:	5	4	3	2	1
2	How do you rate the instructor (preparation, communication, etc.)? Comments:	5	4	3	2	1
3	How do you rate the organization of the course (pacing, length, sequence, etc.)? Comments:	5	4	3	2	1
4	How do you rate the design of the course (exercises, lectures, etc.)? Comments:	5	4	3	2	1
5	How do you rate the course materials (accuracy, clarity, helpfulness, etc.)? Comments:	5	4	3	2	1

sometimes easier said than done. If eleven students say your course was the best training they ever received and one student says you're the worst teacher in the galaxy, which comment will keep you awake that night?)

This is one reason that instructors become frustrated with student evaluations. If three students say the program moved too slowly, you can be sure that three others will say it moved too fast. Since both evaluations are true, it's hard to know whether you should speed up or slow down. Begin by realizing that there is no such thing as an "average" student. If your right hand is plunged into a bucket of ice water while your left receives similar treatment in a bucket of boiling water, I doubt you would describe yourself as "on average" comfortable. In other words, if you simply average the extreme ratings on a questionnaire, they will cancel each other out. Nevertheless, such feedback is still useful. It is probably the naive users who found the training to be too fast and the experienced users who found it to be too slow. One option is to provide more time for individual activity or one-on-one counseling. A second option is to design different exercises for experienced and naive users. Whatever design decision you make, you are better off basing that decision on a careful evaluation of student feedback than on your own best guess.

Follow-Up Evaluations

So far, this has been a discussion of student evaluations that are administered at the end of a course. Such evaluations tell you how students feel immediately after training. If you are interested in learning how students perceive the training once they try to put their new skills to use in the real world, you will have to do a follow-up evaluation (see Exhibit 8.6). Follow-up evaluations are best administered two to six weeks after training. If you wait at least two weeks, learners will have had a chance to test their learning on the job. After six weeks, impressions of the training and its impact have begun to fade.[2]

EXHIBIT 8.6.   Know It All Follow-Up Evaluation.

Now that you have had a chance to put your Know It All training to use, we need your input to determine the effectiveness of the training. Please give us your reactions, and use the back of this form to make additional comments or suggestions.

Instructions: Please circle the appropriate response after each statement.

#	How did you feel about the Know It All training?	Strongly agree	Agree	Neutral	Disagree	Strongly disagree
1	The course prepared me to use Know It All in my work.	5	4	3	2	1
2	I have maintained contact with my "training buddy."	5	4	3	2	1
3	I use Know It All at least three times a week.	5	4	3	2	1
4	I refer to the user guide and job aids when I have a question.	5	4	3	2	1
5	I would recommend this course to other Drummond Beughel partners.	5	4	3	2	1

There are two major problems with follow-up evaluations: they take time to administer and the response rate is generally low. Consider the following techniques to increase the likelihood that people will return a follow-up questionnaire:[3]

• Keep it short. Only ask the questions for which you're sure you'll need answers.

- Include understandable directions.
- Attach a concise cover letter explaining the importance of the survey.
- Make it easy for students to get the survey back to you (E-mail or fax if possible).
- Offer to send a summary of the findings to students who respond.

If a full-scale follow-up evaluation is not feasible but you feel that you would benefit from some feedback, consider using a card similar to the one in Exhibit 8.7. This is actually a postcard, preprinted with your name and address and stamped with the correct postage. Distribute the postcard at the end of class, and ask students to mail it back to you in a month. Since the card only asks one question, it often gets a better response rate than a longer, more complex questionnaire.

EXHIBIT 8.7. Follow-Up Feedback Postcard.

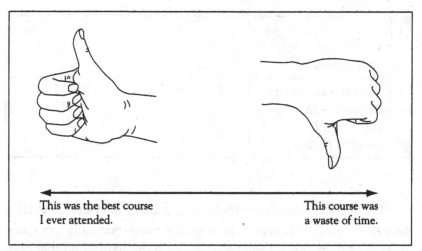

| This was the best course I ever attended. | This course was a waste of time. |

What's Next

Training is a combination of teaching (what *you* do) and learning (what *they* do). This chapter has addressed the issue of how to evaluate teaching. It has recommended using multiple perspectives, including self-assessment, peer review, and student evaluations. While it is useful to evaluate teaching, the ultimate purpose of training is for students to learn. Learning can be defined as the extent to which participants change their attitudes, improve their understanding, and/or increase their skills. Chapter Nine describes methods you can use to discover how much your students learned as a result of your training.

9

Evaluating Learning

Beyond Multiple-Choice Tests

Report from the Trenches: Will This Raptor Fly?

The Gogettum Group is a consulting firm that specializes in improving productivity in financial institutions. Gogettum's major product is a software program called RAPTOR (Real-time Automated Productivity Tracking for Optimal Results) that helps managers improve the overall profitability of their work centers by tracking and analyzing their costs, revenues, outputs, and quality. When banks purchase a RAPTOR site license, Gogettum provides a five-day course that teaches managers how to use the system.

Adam Braiter, president of Jayhawk Bank & Trust in Kansas City, Kansas, is intrigued by RAPTOR. He believes that to remain profitable his bank must do a better job of cost tracking and long-range planning. Being a cautious man, however, Adam does not want to commit bank funds unless he is sure that RAPTOR really makes a difference. He negotiates with Gogettum to run a pilot program for the seven managers in the bank's main office in downtown Kansas City. Adam's plan is to install RAPTOR on each manager's computer, send the seven managers to training, and let them try out RAPTOR in their work centers for three months. He tells Gogettum that if the managers actually learn and use RAPTOR, the bank will go ahead with the site license for the forty-five Jayhawk branches throughout the state of Kansas.

Howie Doone is the training manager at Jayhawk Bank & Trust. His primary responsibility is to oversee training of new tellers and operations staff in the branches. He has just left a meeting with Adam, who has given him a succinct directive: "Howie, I want to know if this RAPTOR training works. Will our managers leave the course with the skills they need to use the program? If they don't learn it, they won't use it. I need some good, solid numbers before I buy into the whole shebang. Make it happen."

Howie doesn't know much about evaluation, but he does know that when Adam Braiter issues an order to jump, the only acceptable response is "How high?" So, Howie goes back to his office, slumps down in his ergonomically correct desk chair, and starts to think about how he can evaluate the RAPTOR pilot program. Eventually, three questions materialize from the tangled muddle of his thoughts:

1. *Why* do I want to evaluate?

2. *What* do I need to evaluate?

3. *How* do I evaluate it?

Why Evaluate?

Why evaluate RAPTOR? Why, indeed. Until Howie figures out the answer to this question, it is pointless for him to spend energy on what and how to evaluate. Too often, organizations evaluate learners for no better reasons than "It's part of our corporate policy" or "We've always done it." Since testing is time-consuming, it only makes sense to do it when the organization will make good use of the data. Or as Neal Whitman, an outstanding educator and evaluator, is fond of saying: "An evaluation not worth doing is not worth doing well." The following are valid reasons to evaluate learner achievement:

1. *When mastery of skills is mandatory.* The goal of training is always learning, of course, but some skills are more equal than others. For example, while it might be nice for the graphics professionals in a public seminar to master the skill of editing Bézier curves, the fate of Western civilization does not depend on their ability to do so. Conversely, a training program for the safety technicians in a nuclear plant had better prove that its graduates can operate the automated monitoring system with 100 percent accuracy. Anything less and the plant may be brought to a screeching halt—or worse. In this situation, evaluation succeeds when it accurately predicts which students will perform adequately on the job.

2. *To gain information on how to improve future courses.* The more wide-reaching the training, the more important it is to evaluate its effectiveness. For example, if once a semester you teach one work-study student how to operate the department's word processor, you can probably get a sense of how well you taught simply by observing the student on the job. If the student keeps running to you for help on setting margins, plan to teach that skill differently next semester. Conversely, suppose you have designed a course that teaches faculty how to use the university's on-line reference system. You plan to offer this one-day course ten times over the next year (and thereafter as needed), so you want to be sure it is effective. By testing the first group of learners, you may discover areas of confusion that you can clarify in future courses. In this situation, evaluation succeeds when it finds things to fix, and especially when it provides some clues about how they should be fixed.

3. *To decide whether to continue or discontinue training.* Some courses are initially offered as pilots. If they bring about the desired results, they are continued; if not, they are either modified or discontinued entirely. For example, the university's end-user computing department decides that you should train just the faculty in the school of engineering how to use the on-line reference system. At the same time, the department tracks system usage in the school of pharmacy and the law school. If usage is about the same in all three schools, the department may conclude that faculty members are

perfectly capable of teaching themselves how to use the system. In this situation, evaluation succeeds when it provides enough good measures to help trainers choose among competing courses or decide whether to continue using an ongoing course.

RAPTOR training falls under the third reason for evaluating because it is a pilot program. Adam Braiter was correct in thinking that if the seven managers at the bank's main office don't learn RAPTOR, they won't use it. Howie wonders if he should simply survey the managers after three months to find out how many of them are using the system. Maybe, he reasons, he can extrapolate backwards: if they aren't using it, then he can assume they didn't learn it. Howie's plan would certainly be less work, but his thinking is erroneous: if managers don't use RAPTOR, it may not be because they don't know how. Any number of variables at the organizational, process, or job level can keep people from doing things they know how to do.[1] Perhaps their subordinates don't have time to gather cost tracking data. Perhaps the managers themselves don't have time to enter these data into RAPTOR and analyze the resulting productivity figures. Perhaps they are afraid that pathetic productivity figures will cost them their jobs.

This is not to say that postcourse behavior should be ignored. But to be meaningful, it should be combined with measures of learner achievement. Now Howie can frame an answer to his first question. He writes it in the form of a mission statement and tacks it on his wall (see Exhibit 9.1).

What to Evaluate

According to Howie's mission statement, the purpose of this evaluation is to "measure how much the seven managers learned during the RAPTOR training pilot." Sounds pretty vague, doesn't it? Let's get a bit more specific by defining learning: *the extent to which participants change attitudes, improve understanding, and/or increase skills as a result of attending the program.*[2] Yikes. If Howie were to measure all that, RAPTOR training would have to be increased from five

EXHIBIT 9.1. Howie's Mission Statement.

> The purpose of this evaluation is to measure how much the seven managers learned during the RAPTOR training pilot. This information, combined with follow-up data that show how often the managers actually use RAPTOR, will help Adam Braiter decide if he wants to implement the system throughout Jayhawk Bank & Trust.

days to six, in order to accommodate all the necessary testing. Adam has said he needs good solid numbers, but clearly a bit of restraint is in order. Chapters Three, Four, and Five of this book dealt with the problem of deciding what to teach, since you can't teach it all. Similarly, you can't—and needn't—evaluate it all. Learner evaluation should be kept lean and mean. What is the least amount of evidence necessary to convince Adam that the managers in the RAPTOR pilot have changed their attitudes, improved their understanding, and increased their skill?

Learner Attitudes

Let's begin with learner attitudes. Chapter Eight discussed the fact that learners invariably have feelings about the teaching process. In addition, learners will leave training with positive or negative attitudes about the system itself. If learners have a positive attitude toward the system, they are more likely to use it and more likely to feel satisfied when they do so. If they have a negative attitude, they are less likely to use the system; or if using the system is a job requirement, they will not be happy campers. Evaluating attitude is tricky: did the training really change learners' opinions of the system, or did they have these opinions right from the start? To answer this question beyond the shadow of a doubt, learners should be surveyed at the beginning and at the end of the training. This may be overkill, but it is worthwhile doing if the main purpose of the training is attitude change. For example, a course in basic computer literacy may be focused more on attitude than on skill, with the goal of helping naive users overcome computer anxiety and get ready to learn on their own. If an end-of-course attitude survey reveals that learners' computer anxiety is low, the course might be deemed a success. However, if the same attitude survey given before training had revealed that the students had no computer anxiety in the first place, the end-of-course survey results would indicate that the course did not have much of an impact on learner attitudes.

If the purpose of evaluation is to improve the training, it may be useful to survey learner attitudes both before and after a course. In the case of RAPTOR training, however, Howie's evaluation mission is not to improve the vendor's training—he simply wants to know if the current program works. What is the least amount of evidence that will convince Adam that managers leave training with a positive attitude toward RAPTOR? Howie knows these managers pretty well: they are used to running their work centers their own way, are suspicious of change, and dislike outside interference. Howie knows that if they dislike RAPTOR, they won't use it. He also realizes that he doesn't have to administer a complicated attitude survey about each part of the system; he just needs to ask them one question on the last day of the course: "Are you willing to try out RAPTOR in your work center?" Asking this question at the start of training is not necessary. Adam Braiter simply needs to know whether his managers' attitudes are positive when training is finished—he doesn't much care how they felt before.

Learner Understanding

In addition to changing attitudes, training can bring about an improvement in understanding. Understanding is a prerequisite to performance: unless computer users know the vocabulary, concepts, and principles of a system, they will only be able to operate the system in a rote way. A major goal of computer-use training should be for people to become independent problem-solvers. Some (fortunately fewer and fewer) computer trainers disagree: they believe that their job is just to tell people how to make the system work, without explaining why. This sort of mindless memorization of steps and procedures, while initially less time-consuming to teach, does not pay off in the long run. When these learners encounter a situation that was not covered during training, they will have no idea how to approach it.

If understanding is a prerequisite to performance, how do you go about testing learners' understanding? I recommend that in most cases you don't. Not that understanding isn't important, but it often does not need to be measured directly. Remember: the goal is a lean and mean evaluation. Consider the RAPTOR training. To master the program, managers need to become familiar with terms like "work center model," "product," and "forecast." They also need to understand core concepts such as the difference between productivity and profitability, and the implications of using each of these measures to do long-range planning. So, what is the least amount of evidence that will convince Adam that managers have learned these terms and concepts? Should Howie develop a test that requires managers to write out a definition of each RAPTOR term, with an extra-credit essay question on the business advantages of measuring profitability? This type of test would certainly indicate how much managers understand, but it wouldn't get to the heart of Howie's mission statement. Remember, Adam Braiter wants to know if managers are able to use RAPTOR. If they can use RAPTOR to perform cost tracking and long-range planning in their own work centers, it is almost certainly because they understand the system's vocabulary, concepts, and principles. Of course, if these managers can't use the system, it may be because they don't understand these things, and if the purpose of this evaluation were to improve the training, Howie would have to find out if this is the case. But Howie doesn't want to improve the vendor's course; he just wants to find out if it works. Consequently, his evaluation will be more efficient if he turns his attention to the third aspect of learning: increased skills.

Learner Skills

Learners may believe that a system will help them do their jobs better, and they may understand the system's basic vocabulary, concepts, and principles; but attitude and understanding are irrelevant if learners can't use the system to accomplish their work. Most computer systems require users to master hundreds of individual skills. Don't make the mistake of thinking that you must evaluate performance on each and every skill. Some skills are prerequisite to others; if learners have mastered the highest-level skill, you can assume they have mastered the ones below it. For example, to set up a work center model in RAPTOR, managers must know how to perform four other procedures: defining work center products, identifying quality measures, creating a time line, and building formulas. Consequently, testing managers' ability to set up a work center model will also test their mastery of these four subordinate procedures. If they are not able to set up a work center, chances are they cannot perform one of the subordinate procedures. But again, it isn't Howie's job to improve the vendor's course; he just wants to find out if it teaches managers the skills they need to use RAPTOR to track costs in their work centers.

How to Evaluate

So far, this chapter has discussed reasons why you might need to evaluate, as well as what kinds of things you should consider evaluating. The next section discusses the "how" of evaluation: techniques you can use to evaluate learner attitude, understanding, and skill.

Evaluating Learner Attitudes

Depending on how you define the purpose of your evaluation, you may decide that it is important to measure learner attitudes in some fashion. These attitudes can be evaluated with written surveys or with interviews. Written surveys have two advantages: they are easy to administer and they are anonymous. Learners are often reluctant to express negative attitudes publicly. They may be concerned that criticism of the training will reflect poorly on themselves, or they may be reluctant to confront the trainer, especially if he or she is a colleague. Conversely, although individual or group interviews take more time and do not provide anonymity, they are a richer source of data than written surveys because learners are not limited to the items on the survey.

Thought/feeling cards are a technique that combines the ease and privacy of a written survey with the open-endedness of an interview. To use this technique, distribute blank index cards to participants at the end of training. The instructions are simple: "On one side of the card, write a sentence that describes how you are thinking about the system. On the other side of the card, write a sentence that describes how you are feeling about the system." The amount of information contained in a simple stack of index cards can be quite astonishing. Exhibit 9.2 shows the responses Howie received from the seven work center managers.

It is clear from these responses that two out of the seven managers are highly resistant to RAPTOR. There is no way of knowing whether they walked into the classroom with chips on their shoulders (though I would suspect they did), but as was said earlier, Howie isn't interested in cause and effect. He doesn't care if training brought about a change in attitude; he just cares whether, by the end of training, the managers think well of the system. Is five out of seven a satisfactory number? If Adam Braiter's ultimate goal is to train more than two hundred managers, and if the seven managers in the pilot program are representative of their counterparts in the branches, then as many as fifty managers could potentially leave training with negative feelings about RAPTOR. Only Adam can decide if 70 percent manager acceptance of RAPTOR is good enough—but Howie has given him helpful information upon which to base that decision.

EXHIBIT 9.2. Responses to Thought/Feeling Cards.

Thoughts	Feelings
This will never work in our department—how can you put a price on customer service?	Ho, hum. Yet another of Adam Hotshot Braiter's wild ideas.
This will be a great way to find out which of my employees are dead weight!	Excited.
This system looks powerful—it will give me information I never had before.	Worried: What happens if my work center shows lousy figures?
I'm going to have to put in lots of extra hours to make this thing work.	Hopeful that the extra time will pay off in the long run.
I have to find some money to hire a temp for the initial data entry—otherwise I'll be putting in too many extra hours.	Optimistic: this may help me run the department better.
I hate this system!!!	I hate this system with a passion!!!!!
This system is really impressive—sort of a "spreadsheet on steroids."	Delighted that the bank is finally making a commitment to profitability. It's about time!

Evaluating Learner Understanding

If you are evaluating a course for the purpose of improving it, you may decide to test for understanding. This chapter has already discussed the fact that in most cases you can extrapolate students' understanding from their mastery of skills: if they can perform the skills, they probably also have the understanding that supports these skills. However, if they have not mastered the skills, you may want to know which concepts they missed so that you can modify the course. In that case, you will need to construct some sort of paper-

and-pencil test, using the appropriate mix of multiple-choice, true-false, fill-in-the-blank, matching, and essay questions. It is beyond the scope of this book to cover the procedures for constructing and validating such tests, but a number of excellent books exist on the subject of test construction.[3]

Evaluating Learner Skills

Depending on how you define the purpose of your evaluation, chances are you will conclude that some measure of learner skill is important. The following three guidelines can help you develop efficient and effective performance tests:

1. *Make the test relevant.* Since a system can potentially require learners to master hundreds of new skills, it is important to evaluate the skills that are most critical for these learners. For example, it is a waste of time to test managers on their ability to enter daily production figures into RAPTOR if this task will be performed by a secretary.

2. *Make the test specific.* There is a delicate balance between items that are so specific as to be trivial and those that are so global as to be unmeasurable. A spoof of the M.I.T. Graduate Qualifying Examination in Philosophy illustrates the latter case: "Sketch the development of human thought; estimate its significance. Compare with the development of any other kind of thought."[4] A RAPTOR performance test that simply instructs managers to "use RAPTOR to track your costs" is less helpful than a test that breaks down this behavior into three or four critical skills and measures the achievement of each.

3. *Make the test useful for feedback.* A test should help students clearly see whether their performance was on target. Everyone has had the experience of getting back a final exam and, whether the news was good or bad, having no idea how the teacher arrived at the grade. In a well-designed performance test, this type of confusion should not occur. For example,

during RAPTOR training, managers could be given a sample work center with a year's worth of data and asked to do a "what if" forecast for the next year. If the numbers look reasonable, managers will know they did the forecasting correctly. If the numbers look peculiar, both they and the instructor will know they have a problem, and the instructor will be able to help them figure out what went wrong.

Pretesting

Whether you are evaluating attitudes, understanding, or skill, pretesting is occasionally useful. In this evaluation design, students are given a survey or test before training begins and are then given the same (or a similar) test at the end of training. Pretesting is controversial. Many computer trainers consider it a waste of time, since students typically don't attend computer-use training unless they need it. This is a good point: if RAPTOR is a brand-new program for Jayhawk Bank, it is safe to assume that managers would score a perfect zero on a pretest of RAPTOR skills and concepts. In this case, a posttest alone would measure whether they have learned. However, pretesting can be useful if you are trying out a new training design and you want to demonstrate that the new approach works. It can also be a helpful technique if you suspect that learners already possess the information being taught. For example, if the vendor's RAPTOR course spends the first eight hours of the course teaching general computer concepts and if Howie believes that this is a waste of a training day because the managers already understand and use computers, he may want to test out his theory by administering a brief pretest before training and administering the same test at the end of training. If this demonstrates that the managers had a 90 percent understanding when they arrived in class and a 95 percent understanding when they left, Howie (and Adam) might well question whether Jayhawk Bank is getting its money's worth from this part of the vendor's course. Pretesting may also be useful if attitude change is a major training goal. For example, if an organization perceives that its employees are resistant to office automation and the training department has developed a course to convince them that technology is their friend, it would be useful to survey their attitudes before and after training to determine if training had a positive impact.

When to Evaluate

In addition to deciding *how* to evaluate, it is important to decide *when* the evaluation should take place. Learners are typically tested immediately after training is over, but there are other options. Testing can occur throughout a training session. This is especially useful during long courses, to give students feedback while they are still being trained. For example, each RAPTOR lesson could end with a mini-exercise that lets the instructor evaluate how well the managers grasped the skills presented that day. Managers who have trouble completing the exercise could be given an extra assignment to complete as homework before the next morning's session begins.

Attitudes and skills can also be evaluated after the course is over. Once learners are back on the job, however, the emphasis shifts from attitudes and skills to *behavior*. Ultimately, change in behavior is the goal of any training program. In other words, to what extent do participants do things differently on the job because they attended training? While you may not be in a position to evaluate behavioral change, it is important to realize that simply testing learners at the end of a course does not show whether they will use the information once they leave. A follow-up evaluation such as the one shown in Exhibit 9.3 might tell Howie whether managers are actually using RAPTOR to track costs in their work centers. It is also important to realize that if a follow-up evaluation indicates that behavior has not changed, the training may or may not be at fault. For behavior change to occur, four conditions are necessary:[5]

1. The person must know what to do and how to do it.

2. The person must have a desire to change.

3. The person must work in the right climate.

4. The person must be rewarded for changing.

Only the first of these conditions is within your control as a trainer. This may make you feel a bit bleak: despite your best efforts, you still may not have the impact you hoped for. However, while you can't do it alone, you are essential to the process. Teaching people what to do and how to do it is your job, and without it, behavior change is well-nigh impossible.

EXHIBIT 9.3. RAPTOR Follow-Up Evaluation.

Now that you have had a chance to put your RAPTOR training to use, we need your input to determine how well the training worked. Please let us know which RAPTOR functions you are using. *Instructions: Please check the appropriate box after each statement. Write additional comments or suggestions in the last column.*

#	What have you done so far?	Yes	No	N/A	Comments:
1	I have set up the RAPTOR model of my work center.	☐	☐	☐	
2	I have collected cost, revenue, output, and quality data.	☐	☐	☐	
3	I have entered cost, revenue, output, and quality data into RAPTOR.	☐	☐	☐	
4	I have used RAPTOR to generate productivity tracking reports.	☐	☐	☐	
5	I have used RAPTOR to create work center forecasts.	☐	☐	☐	

What's Next

It is a pity that in a book about teaching, the chapters about evaluation must come last. Logically, of course, this sequence makes sense. After all, that's what happens in the real world: first you decide what to teach, then you teach it, and finally, to be sure it worked, you evaluate. Following this sequence in a book, however, practically guarantees that the evaluation chapters will be either skimmed or skipped entirely. This is reminiscent of what goes on in high school American History classes, or at least what went on in the 1960s when I was there to observe it. The first half of the year is spent on explorers, colonization, the Revolutionary War, and the Constitution. The War of 1812 coincides with Valentine's Day. Then comes the Civil War, and suddenly it's May—with approximately four weeks to cover the entire twentieth century.

I hope that the placement of Chapters Eight and Nine has not led you to conclude that evaluation is any less important than the other information in this book. Evaluating outcomes should not be an afterthought; it should be an integral part of the process. And as Figure 9.1

FIGURE 9.1. A Blueprint for Computer Training.

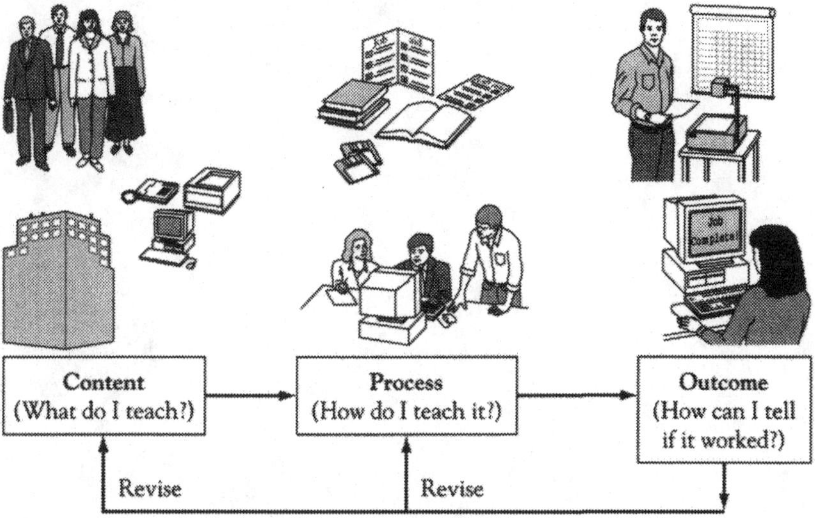

| Content (What do I teach?) | Process (How do I teach it?) | Outcome (How can I tell if it worked?) |

Revise   Revise

shows, after evaluation comes revision. Depending on what you discover when you evaluate teaching and learning, you may decide that you should revise the *content* (what you taught) and/or the *process* (how you taught it). Take another look at your needs assessments of the learners (Chapter Three), the system (Chapter Four), and the work environment (Chapter Five). Are you satisfied that what you taught was what people most needed to learn? Check out your teaching methods (Chapter Six) and support materials (Chapter Seven). Is there anything you could do better next time? Be alert to opportunities for improvement.

What's next? What's next is in your most capable hands.

Notes

Preface

1. Greenberg, D. *How to Be a Jewish Mother.* Garden City, NY: Doubleday, 1965.

2. Gupta, U. "TV Seminars and CD-ROMs Train Workers." *The Wall Street Journal,* January 3, 1996, p. B1.

3. Bach, F. T. "Brancusi: The Reality of Sculpture." In T. P. Friedrich, F. T. Bach, M. Rowell, and A. Temkin (Eds.), *Constantin Brancusi.* Philadelphia: Philadelphia Museum of Art, 1995, p. 23.

Chapter One

1. National Society for Performance and Instruction. *News & Notes,* January 1995, p. 6.

2. Kirkpatrick, D. "Making It All Worker-Friendly." *Fortune,* 1993, *128*(7), 44–53.

3. Galitz, W. O. *User-Interface Screen Design.* Boston: QED Publishing Group, 1993, p. 2.

4. Fox, R. "Newstrack." *Communications of the ACM,* 1995, *38*(7), p. 9.

5. Drucker, P. G. "The Age of Social Transformation." *Atlantic Monthly,* 1994, *274,* 53–80.

6. Compeau, D., Olfman, L., Sei, M., and Webster, J. "End-User Training and Learning." *Communications of the ACM*, 1995, *38*(7), 24–26.

Chapter Three

1. Weiss, E. *Making Computers People-Literate*. San Francisco: Jossey-Bass, 1994.

Chapter Four

1. Schneiderman, B. *Designing the User Interface: Strategies for Effective Human-Computer Interaction*. Reading, Mass.: Addison-Wesley, 1992.

2. Weiss, E. *Making Computers People-Literate*.

Chapter Five

1. McConnell, V., and Koch, K. *Computerizing the Corporation: The Intimate Link Between People and Machines*. New York: Van Nostrand Reinhold, 1990.

2. Carlisle, K. *Analyzing Jobs and Tasks*. Englewood Cliffs, N.J.: Educational Technology Publications, 1986.

3. Eason, K. D. "Understanding the Naive Computer User." *The Computer Journal*, 1975, *19*(1), 3–7.

Chapter Six

1. Mayhew, D. J. *Principles and Guidelines in Software User Interface Design*. Englewood Cliffs, N.J.: Prentice-Hall, 1992.

2. Stepich, D. "From Novice to Expert: Implications for Instructional Design." *Performance & Instruction*, 1991, *30*(6), 13–17.

3. Norman, D. "What Goes On in the Mind of the Learner." *New Directions for Teaching and Learning*, 1980, *2*, 37–49.

4. Mayer, R. E. "The Psychology of How Novices Learn Computer Programming." *Computer Surveys*, 1981, *13*(1), 121–141.

5. Moran, T. P. "Getting into a System: External-Internal Task Mapping Analysis." *Proceedings of the Computer-Human Interaction (CHI) Conference on Human Factors in Computing*, Boston, April 24–28, 1983, pp. 45–49.

6. Kerka, S. "On Second Thought: Using New Cognitive Research in Vocational Education." *ERIC Digest*, 1987, 53.

7. Knowles, M. *The Modern Practice of Education*. New York: Association Press, 1970.

8. Schwenk, T., and Whitman, N. *Residents as Teachers: A Guide to Educational Practice* (2nd ed.). Salt Lake City: University of Utah School of Medicine, 1993.

9. Laird, D. *Approaches to Training and Development*. Reading, Mass.: Addison-Wesley, 1978.

10. Powers, B. *Instructor Excellence: Mastering the Delivery of Training*. San Francisco: Jossey-Bass, 1992.

11. Broad, M., and Newstrom, J. *Transfer of Training*. Reading, Mass.: Addison-Wesley, 1992.

Chapter Seven

1. Horton, W. *Designing and Writing Online Documentation: Help Files to Hypertext*. New York: Wiley, 1990.

2. Rossett, A., and Gautier-Downes, J. *A Handbook of Job Aids*. San Diego, Calif.: Pfeiffer, 1991.

3. Stolovitch, H., and Vanasse, S. "The Paradox of User Documentation: Useful But Rarely Used." *Performance & Instruction*, August 1989, pp. 19–22.

4. Stolovitch and Vanasse, "The Paradox of User Documentation," pp. 19–22.

5. Gropper, G. L. "How Text Displays Add Value to Text Content." *Educational Technology*, 1988, 28(4), 15–21.

6. Glynn, S. M., Britton, B. K., and Tillman, M. H. "Typographical Cues in Text: Management of the Reader's Attention." In D. H. Jonassen (Ed.), *The Technology of Text*. Englewood Cliffs, N.J.: Educational Technology Publications, 1985, pp. 192–209.

7. Hartley, J. "Planning the Typographical Structure of Instructional Text." *Educational Psychologist*, 1986, *22*(4), 315–332.

8. Rossett and Gautier-Downes, *A Handbook of Job Aids*.

9. Horton, W. "Let's Do Away with Manuals . . . Before They Do Away with Us. *Technical Communication*, Jan.–Mar. 1993, pp. 26–34.

Chapter Eight

1. Kirkpatrick, D. *Evaluating Training Programs: The Four Levels.* San Francisco: Berrett-Koehler, 1994.

2. Masie, E., and Wolman, R. *The Computer Training Handbook.* Raquette Lake, N.Y.: National Training & Computers Project, 1988.

3. Kosecoff, J., and Fink, A. *Evaluation Basics: A Practitioners Manual.* Beverly Hills, Calif.: Sage, 1982.

Chapter Nine

1. Rummler, G., and Brache, A. *Improving Performance: How to Manage the White Space on the Organization Chart.* San Francisco: Jossey-Bass, 1990.

2. Kirkpatrick, D. *Evaluating Training Programs.*

3. Kosecoff, J., and Fink, A. *Evaluation Basics: A Practitioners Manual.* Thousand Oaks, Calif.: Sage, 1982; Morris, L., and Fitz-Gibbon, C. *How To Measure Achievement.* Thousand Oaks, Calif.: Sage, 1978; Kirkpatrick, D. *Evaluating Training Programs.*

4. Novak, W., and Waldoks, M. *The Big Book of New American Humor.* New York: Harper Perrennial, 1990, p. 94.

5. Kirkpatrick, D. *Evaluating Training Programs*, p. 23.

Index